# Personal Financial Management

**First Edition**

Manufactured in the United States of America

ISBN: 0991567900
ISBN 13: 9780991567904

1. Personal Finances  2. Self Help  3. Financial Security 4. Debt Management

Published by Eagle One Resources, LLC

Edited by Denise McCabe, McCabe Editing

www.mccabeediting.com

# Personal Financial Management

## *The toolkit they never gave you in school*

by

**Tom Hoisington**
**CLU, ChFC, FICF**

# DEDICATION

This book is dedicated to the two men who had the most profound influence on my life.

Ezra E. Hoisington, my father, who taught me about life; about loving family. You lived your life in a manner that was a textbook example of what a husband and father should be.

Raymond E. Mazy, my first agency manager and mentor, who shared all that he knew with only one condition...that we must share the knowledge that he shared with us, and all that we would learn from life as well, with others that their lives might be improved.

Dad, Ray, this book is for you.

# Acknowledgments

I have been blessed with a multitude of friends and business associates, whose help has been priceless in many ways.

Thank you, Jeannie Anderson, President of LifeSigns.us in Tennessee. You have been, at various times, a coach and mentor; a patient listener who helped me see when the glass was half full rather than half empty; a visionary who encouraged me to pursue a passion; and, most of all, a very good friend.

To my longtime friend in South Carolina, Robert "Father Bob" Donovan, who provided me with my first real opportunity to help author a book, thank you. You helped me discover a gift that I did not realize I possessed.

To Denise McCabe at McCabe Editing, I cannot thank you enough for all of your guidance and suggestions. You have made this so much better than I could have hoped.

A special thanks to all of the members of the Central Florida Chapter of the National Speakers Association. Each of you has provided insight, encouragement, and straightforward critiques that have "told it like it is." Thank you for sharing your wisdom and experience as we journey together on the road we know as public speaking.

Finally, to my wife of 33 years, Lin, thank you for understanding during all those days and nights when I locked myself away with the computer. Through thick and thin, you have always been beside me offering encouragement and support. No man could ever have asked for, nor been given, a better or more supportive partner.

# Table of Contents

# Introduction

Decade in and decade out, through good times and bad, American families have struggled with their personal finances. For some, the problems were created by overwhelming debts incurred on the assumption that annual incomes would continue to increase, the stock market would continue to go up, and home values would continue to escalate. Others suddenly found themselves without employment due to the "outsourcing" of their jobs to foreign lands where wages are lower. Those who were still employed were suddenly faced with stagnant wages and ever increasing costs of living.

Many people held the belief that there was no need to plan for the future—no real need to make certain that full value was obtained for every dollar spent. The lessons learned by our parents, grandparents, and great-grandparents during the years of the Great Depression of the 1930s faded from memory and were merely the stuff of history books. New generations took for granted that "it can't happen to us."

The advent of the Great Recession of late 2007 has changed that line of thought and that perception of life. Today individuals and families alike are looking for ways to coax the maximum value from every dollar. They look for guidance from the previously ignored lessons of their predecessors who lived through the Great Depression of the 1930s. Those who are still alive from that time share their insights—"think twice before you spend your money"..."save for a rainy day"..."don't take on more debt than you can pay back"..."be smart with your money."

The *good news* contained in this book is that being smart with our money is not as difficult as it sometimes appears. The American people have demonstrated time and again that we can be, and are, resilient; that given the right information, we can make wise spending decisions and provide for ourselves.

This book contains basic information that each of us needs to become good stewards of our financial resources, to make wise budgeting and spending decisions, and to plan for our futures. It makes the seemingly complex, simple and understandable. It is based on my experiences working with thousands of families from all walks of life who each wanted to retake control of their finances, to pay off debts, to spend wisely, to save and build a bright future. In the final analysis, they all wanted the same thing: the tools that would empower them to obtain the best values for their hard-earned dollars.

This book is intended to give you those tools. Chapters 1 - 4 will focus on income—where your money comes from and where it can be stored for future use. Chapters 5 - 6 focus on basic living expenses. Chapters 7 - 10 address managing the risks that are inherent in daily life. Finally, chapters 11 - 14 help you develop plans for long-term financial security. Let's get started!

# Personal Financial Management

## The toolkit they never gave you in school

by

**Tom Hoisington**
**CLU, ChFC, FICF**

*"Can anybody remember when the times were not hard and money not scarce?"*

- Ralph Waldo Emerson

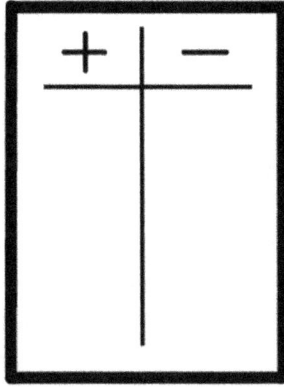

## CHAPTER 1

# Budget

*The Four-Letter Word That Should Be Used in EVERY House*

"We must consult our means rather than our wishes."

— George Washington

Let's face it. If there were any justice in this world, wouldn't "budget" be a four-letter word? People don't like to be told that they cannot do whatever they want to with the money that they've worked so hard to earn. So, let's replace the word "budget" with a nicer, kinder four-letter word: Plan. A spending plan.

When we use a spending plan to manage money, what we do is thought out in advance. There is a plan for every dollar—even the fun ones—and by following the plan, those dollars are applied *exactly* where they are most needed.

To build this plan, there are some things that have to be considered. We will begin with how much money there is to work with and where it comes from. This, then, is our starting point: income.

## Income and Deductions

Have you ever noticed that when people talk about income, they always talk about the gross pay, the money in the check before any deductions are taken, instead of net income, the amount left after deductions have been taken from the paycheck? Have you also noticed that people also tend to have overly optimistic expectations when they begin the budgeting process? As a financial counselor, I've seen many people attempt to create their budget with the expectation that there will *always* be overtime pay and that they will never experience a reduction in work to be done or hours to be worked.

Sadly, this can be a big mistake. Overtime is seldom guaranteed. Economic downturns happen and income is reduced. Just one week without the extra money can totally derail the best intentioned plan. Perhaps the wisest advice ever given to someone creating a budget is "Underestimate your income and overestimate your expenses. At the end of the month, the worst thing that can happen is you've either made too much money or you haven't spent enough. Neither can hurt you."

When all taxes have been withheld, all benefits paid for, and retirement planned for, the money that remains in the paycheck is ours to spend as we wish. This is where planning and prioritization comes into play.

## Expenses

Generally speaking, one way to categorize expenses is to divide them into one of three categories: fixed, variable, and periodic.

Fixed expenses are those that basically remain the same from one month to the next. Recurring expenditures such as mortgage and rent payments, car payments, real estate taxes, and insurance premiums typically fall into this category.

Variable expenses can change from month to month. Expenses such as food, electricity, and gas fit this description.

Periodic expenses are those that generally do not occur every month. Rather, they occur once every few months, annually, or occasionally. These are the ones that require foresight to be prepared for.

Another way to think of expenses is to divide them into the classes of essential and discretionary expenses.

Essential expenses are those that we cannot live without—the "gotta-have-its." Food, water, shelter, and utilities are all essential items. Survival without them is dicey at best.

Discretionary expenses are those that we can choose to spend our cash on, or not.

## Essential Expenses

## Savings

In most households, savings is placed at the very end of the discretionary spending list. It's as though the driving philosophy behind the budget (if there is one) is "spend on everything we want, and then, if anything is left, we'll put it into savings until we find something else to buy." In other words, it's not really saved money; it's deferred spending. By making savings their lowest priority, these folks have chosen to put themselves last in line for their own money.

On the other hand, when households have a plan for managing their money, they put savings at the top of the list, and it is an essential item. This money is set aside to pay anticipated future expenses and to meet unexpected opportunities or crises.

What each family needs is a Wholly Account. This is a portion of the savings account that is wholly dedicated to meeting anticipated future expenses. For example, let's say license plates on the car must be renewed annually. If the renewal is going to cost $240, then the family needs to set aside $20 every month in order to pay this bill when it comes due.

The same family also needs an Emergency Fund. This is a portion of the savings account that is committed to paying the unexpected expenses that have a way of appearing at the least convenient time. An example of this type of expense might be an auto repair bill.

While there are many "rules of thumb" for how much a family should put into savings, the best strategy is to determine actual needs. As we develop our budget below, we'll pose questions that should be asked to determine how much money needs to be set aside into the Wholly Account and how much into the Emergency Fund.

## Shelter

Perhaps the most important recurring "gotta-have-it" is the rent or mortgage payment. Shelter is one of our most basic needs. Whether it's the monthly mortgage or the rent, timely payment is absolutely imperative. Foreclosure and eviction are not only unhappy, they have many and broad long-term consequences.

## Food and Household Supplies

Equally important is our daily bread. No matter who we are or how old we are, it seems like hunger strikes at least three times a day. Consequently, we need to find ways to manage this expense and save money wherever possible.

While we'll explore this topic in greater detail in Chapter 5, "Fine Dining on a Budget," suffice it to say, prior planning is the key to controlling this expense.

## Utilities

### Water

Clearly, some utilities are "gotta-have-its." First among these is water. While water is a "must have," there are steps that can be taken to control its cost.

To avoid the added cost of bottled drinking water, buy a filter and pitcher to filter tap water. Even with the cost of replacement filters, it's far less expensive than buying bottled water and has the added benefit of reducing the plastic waste we put into landfills.

Another step to control the cost of water is simple conservation. To reduce water consumption, install flow restrictor shower heads and low flow toilets. When washing clothes, avoid partial loads by waiting until a full load needs washing. If a faucet drips, install new washers. We'll talk more about water in Chapter 5.

### Electricity and Other Power

Another essential utility is electricity. Again, conservation is a first line of defense against excessive spending. Turn off lights in empty rooms. Wash clothes in warm or cold water rather than in hot. Turn thermostats down in winter and turn them up in summer. This saves on both power consumption and wear and tear on heating and air conditioning equipment.

One possibility that should be investigated to control monthly expenditures is to determine if the local electric company offers a levelized billing program. Sometimes referred to as "budget plans," these use various means to determine an average billing amount that is paid each month. To illustrate, let's assume that the electric company adds the last twelve months of electric bills and divides by twelve to arrive at an "average" bill of $100 per month. The consumer pays the same amount ($100) each month until the average is recalculated. While it is likely that this will result in overpayments based on usage in some months, it will also result in underpayment in other months. The advantage is simply that the electric bill is now a known factor in planning each month's expenses.

With the exception of turning off lights in empty rooms, the same conservation steps can be taken to manage the cost of natural gas and propane.

## Television and Bundled Services

Many families purchase cable and satellite television services. In some areas, this is purely a luxury, while in others it is an absolute necessity. The key to controlling the cost of service is to separate the necessities from the luxuries and purchase only those services that are absolutely essential. While bundled services—that is, cable television, Internet access, and telephone service—may save money in some instances, there will be other times when purchasing these services separately will result in cost savings.

## Telephone

Finally, telephone service is another utility that provides opportunities for saving money. Consumers who have land lines should closely examine their bills to determine if they are paying for packaged services that they do not use. Those who use cell phones should determine if they are using all of the minutes that they pay for. More and more of those who have both a land line and cellular service are considering whether they truly need both.

One final note regarding telephone service, specifically long-distance service. Many people now use calling cards or pre-paid long-distance cards for their long-distance calling needs. Consumers who use this service will want to determine how much long-distance calling they use, the amount it costs, and how frequently the card must be replenished, so that money can be reserved each month for the cost of refilling the card.

## Transportation

The first transportation cost is the purchase of the vehicle, a subject we will explore in Chapter 4.

Let's face it, cars don't run on hopes and dreams; they require gasoline. So, after the vehicle purchase, this is the first transportation cost to plan. Determine how much fuel must be purchased each week, and make certain that sufficient cash is available to pay for it.

Keeping a car on the road every day requires proper care. Auto maintenance includes not only routine oil changes but replacement of tires, brakes, batteries, hoses, and much more. While few vehicles need upkeep every month, money should be set aside so that the cash is available to pay for these bills when they occur.

Another cost of keeping a car on the road is the annual license plate or registration fee. Whether your state charges modest fees or high fees, this is another example of an expense that can be covered by depositing money each month into the Wholly Account.

Another consideration is the cost of using toll roads. In some places, it is possible to travel across the entire state without ever seeing a toll booth. In other places, it is impossible to drive across town without paying tolls.

A participant in a budget counseling class told her counselor, "My family doesn't have to worry about the toll roads anymore. We have one of those little box thingies hanging on the windshield." The box she was referring to was a *pre-paid* tolls transponder. Obviously, the family must still put money in the budget to replenish the transponder when it is low on funds. Knowing how much money must be put into the box and how often it must be refilled will enable the family to plan the appropriate allocation in the monthly budget.

## Insurance

Insurance is purchased as protection from the vagaries of adverse fortune. When something goes wrong, insurance allows us to "fix it" without necessarily having to take money out of our own pockets. While some insurance policies are required by law (auto insurance) or by a lender (homeowners insurance), others are optional. Required or optional, insurance plays a very key role in helping families manage foreseeable risks and protect against them.

Some premiums are due and payable on a monthly basis. Others are paid quarterly, semi-annually, or annually. All of them can be covered by monthly deposits into the Wholly Account. Money must be built into the budget for the financial well-being of the family.

We will investigate various types of insurance in depth later on. For now, let's just note that insurance is essential and that money must be reserved each month to pay for the protection insurance affords.

## Medical Care

No one can predict who will get sick, or when. Consequently, some people believe that it is not possible to plan for this expense. However, there are steps that can be taken in anticipation of probable medical costs. Proper planning becomes especially important if a worker is having money withheld from his or her paycheck and deposited into a Flexible Healthcare Spending Account. So how does someone plan for this?

Begin by looking back to previous years. How many doctor visits have been made each year by each member of the family? What does each office visit cost? Does a family member take prescription medication on a daily basis? If so, what does each prescription cost? Is there an annual deductible that must be met? Does someone take a daily over-the-counter medication such as vitamins, allergy medications, or daily aspirin?

To illustrate, let's assume a family of four: two adults and two children. Each family member has an annual check-up. The Patient Protection and Affordable Care Act (ACA), which was signed into law in 2010, requires that these annual preventive care exams be covered 100 percent by the family's health insurance policy. Thus, there is no co-pay required. On the other hand, the children typically each see a physician for the normal childhood colds and the flu three times each year; since these are not preventive care exams, each visit requires a $25 co-pay. One family member takes a prescription medication that has a monthly co-pay of $10. When added up, this "average" family spends $270 each year in medical expenses. When divided by twelve, we find that the family must set aside a minimum of $22.50 each month ($270÷12 = $22.50) for a known, repeated expense.

## Clothing

It could go without saying that clothing is essential, but let's talk about it anyway. The types of clothing will depend on what is appropriate to the climate, environment, and activities you and your family engage in. For many families, back-to-school shopping is an annual ritual at the end of summer vacations. For simplicity, we will assume that this is the only time when clothes are purchased—though it's not a realistic assumption. If each of our two children requires $300 worth of new clothing each year, a total of $600 will be spent, so $50 must be placed into the Wholly Account monthly in order to pay for these clothes.

Obviously, children grow during the school year, shoes wear out, and parents need appropriate clothing for work, so once-a-year shopping trips may not be enough for a family. Nonetheless, setting adequate money aside each month prepares the family finances for these expenses regardless of how often new clothing must be purchased.

One money-saving idea came from a friend who had two daughters in high school. As the father of a son, I had no idea how expensive it is to have two daughters going to the prom. This mom took both girls to a consignment shop where each purchased a gown. A seam let out here, another taken in there, and both girls went to prom looking like a million dollars for a fraction of the cost of buying new dresses.

Another good practice is to buy clothing at factory outlets. In some cases, the clothing may have minor flaws that do not affect their appearance or wearability. In others, they are simply products that were produced in too large a quantity. In either case, they are frequently sold for far less than identical items in the big department stores.

### Child Care

Child care includes the cost of day care for pre-schoolers, pre-K classes for children getting a head start to their formal education, and after school care for children who require supervision between the end of the school day and the arrival of a parent.

### Laundry and Dry Cleaning

Clean clothing is a must. While many items can be washed at home, others require dry cleaning. Properly maintained, clothing can last a long time.

If a washer and dryer are available at home, the cost of laundry is two-fold: the short-term cost of buying detergent and paying the monthly water bill, and the long-term cost of repairing or replacing the appliances. If the consumer goes to a commercial Laundromat, money must be planned to drop into the coin slots on the washers and dryers.

## Discretionary Expenses

### Food

Although food is certainly an essential expense, there are elements of food that are purely discretionary.

Working a full day, every day, often leaves little time for meal preparation. While buying prepared foods is convenient, they often cost more than buying the ingredients and preparing the meal yourself.

After a hard day at work, everyone is tired, hungry, and looking for a treat. After all, people have worked hard all day; they've earned a reward. For many, the reward is dining out. Whether the meal is served in a fast food drive-through or a sit-down meal in a restaurant, it's fun to be pampered while someone serves you whatever you choose to eat.

The problem, of course, is that there are costs we may not think about. The restaurant must pay for the ingredients of the meal. Then, it's got to pay someone to cook it, and someone else to serve it. After you've left, yet another person will be paid to wash the dishes and mop the floor. Of course, the restaurant owner also has to pay the rent, the power bill, the water bill, and all the other costs of occupying the building; and, the owner also wants to make a profit.

Obviously, the meal costs far more at the restaurant than it costs at home for lots of reasons.

## Telephone

Once a possession of only the wealthy, the telephone soon expanded its reach until nearly every home had not just one telephone, but an extension in practically every room.

Today, many families have not only the landline telephones in their homes but cell phones as well, and maybe one for each family member. The duplication of services often puts stress on household budgets.

As we mentioned before, as the capabilities of cell phones grow, more and more people will make the decision to have only one telephone again: most often it's their cell phone.

## Clothing

Similar to food, listing clothing under discretionary spending may seem a bit odd! Clothing is definitely a necessity—anyone who has looked in a mirror has seen how nicely clothing hides flaws.

The "discretionary" designation comes from the fact that it is not necessary to own and wear the latest fad or the most expensive name brands.

## Personal Grooming

While some personal grooming items are clearly necessities—think soap, shampoo, toothbrushes and toothpaste, and hairbrushes and combs—others are nice to have but their absence will not kill.

As a guy, I make no pretense of understanding the need for manicures and pedicures. For many women these small luxuries are the ultimate reward, while for other women they are part of a professional image. When the family budget has enough surplus to afford these services, there is no harm in this type of spending. But when money is tight, women may choose to invest in their own bottle of nail polish and emery boards.

The same can be said for haircuts and hair colors. Some individuals spend large sums of money to have hair professionally styled and colored. Others seek out bargains by using the services offered at hair styling schools and/or purchasing products that can be used at home.

## Laundry

Once again, clean clothes are essential. There is no denying this. The "discretionary" designation arises when someone is debating the use of professional laundry services. For example, some men prefer having dress shirts professionally laundered, though they may be less happy when their shirts are returned with buttons missing or broken and creases ironed into the wrong places.

Today, many dress shirts are permanent press and, when hung up immediately after drying, require no ironing at all. When pressing is required, an investment in a steam iron and ironing board will quickly be recouped. Who gets to do the ironing may or may not depend on who does the wearing.

### Charitable Donations

There is an old Arab proverb that states, "If you have much, give of your wealth; if you have little, give of your heart." There is no denying that the world is full of people less fortunate than each of us and who need help. The desire to help the less fortunate is perhaps one of the greatest traits that set mankind apart from all other life forms. Having said that, we recognize that "charity begins at home," including donations to our own religious institutions and to medical research that could benefit members of our own families.

However, the reality is that, no matter how much money someone has, there is a finite number of dollars to work with each month. When a dollar has been used for some purpose, it cannot be used again for another purpose. Therefore, when someone chooses to make a charitable donation, it must be done with the acknowledgment that spending for something else must be either already accounted for or eliminated. It's all a matter of prioritization.

## Memberships

Memberships are a curious form of expense. In some cases they are absolutely indispensable; and in other cases they are quite optional and no harm can arise from their absence.

For example, membership in a professional organization can be essential in order to increase earnings or create opportunities for professional growth. In this case, the expense of joining and remaining a member of the professional organization is, in fact, an investment in career growth.

On the other hand, some memberships can be considered non-essential. A membership in a health club, for example, might be very nice; however, it is not necessary to belong to one in order to exercise and remain physically fit.

## Techniques for Controlling Spending

Looking back at my childhood, I can clearly see my mother sitting in the middle of her bed with envelopes spread around her. There were envelopes for the electric bill, the water bill, the grocery store—an envelope for each necessary expenditure. She took my father's pay and divided it among the envelopes. When she went to the grocery store, she took the grocery envelope to the market along with her shopping list. She kept track of the cost of everything she put into her cart and, when she was at the end of the money in the envelope, she *had* to be at the end of the shopping list.

Today, there are many different ways to keep track of personal budgets and fund allocations. Some still use envelopes; others use one of the wide variety of computer programs. It matters not one bit what the system is. The essential thing is that each family finds a system that works for them and sticks with it.

Budget and financial counselors frequently hear clients ask, "How do I know how much to budget for each expense?" Perhaps the best way to answer this question is for each family member to carry a small spiral notebook (think pocket-size) for 90 days and write down every penny that is spent and what it is spent on. At the end of that time, divide all of the expenditures into budget categories and see where all the money really went. After you review the numbers, if you don't like what they are telling, you have now identified the areas for change. It becomes a simple—though maybe not easy—matter of changing spending habits.

## Conclusion

In the beginning of this chapter, we decided that "budget" is, in fact, a four-letter word. It's a plan that empowers us to prepare for the expenses we face. As we set up our spending plan, there are certain key elements that must be taken into account.

- While our gross income may sound more impressive, we can spend only the net income, the money left after deductions have been taken from the paycheck.

- Expenses generally fall into one of three categories: (1) fixed expenses which remain the same month after month, (2) variable expenses that vary from one month to the next, and (3) periodic expenses that occur only occasionally.

- Within our expenses, there are "gotta-have-its" like shelter, food, water, and electricity, and there are "wanna-have-its" like eating in restaurants, having both cell phones and land lines, and some club memberships.

- In order for savings to happen, it must be given a high priority in the spending plan, if not the #1 position on the list.

- Finally, each of us must find a system for controlling spending that works for us. Be it as simple as envelopes for each expense item or as sophisticated as a computer program, a system helps us stick to the plan.

A budget is simply a plan for the use of money, a plan that empowers us to set financial goals for ourselves. The plan takes into account what is essential in life and what is desirable but not necessary. Laying out our financial priorities and objectives enables us to reach those financial goals.

## CHAPTER 2

# Saving For...

*Being Prepared for Whatever the Fates May Have in Store*

"Thrift comes too late when you find it at the bottom of your purse."

— Seneca

If we had a crystal ball that revealed what was in our future, both good and bad, it would be easy to be financially prepared for whatever was going to happen. Unfortunately, most of us do not have a crystal ball and must plan for the future without seeing it first. How do we do this? We save.

As noted in Chapter 1, if we make savings our last priority, we seldom, if ever, get around to it. This is why "savings" is listed as the first expense on our budget form.

## What Am I Saving For?

Everyone has a unique list of purposes for saving, even if some haven't been given much thought. Let's look at some common reasons why people set money aside.

- **Emergencies**—what would you do if your car broke down tomorrow? Where would you find the money to pay for the repairs? An emergency fund can form the basis for what is, in effect, a savings program. It empowers the saver to be prepared for whatever might happen, both the predictable and the unpredictable.

  In financial planning circles, the recommendation is usually to accumulate multiple months of actual living expenses in an emergency fund. The idea is to determine how many months you could function without an income and still pay all normal living expenses. While this is good advice, for most people the mere thought of trying to accumulate thousands of dollars in savings can be so overwhelming that it paralyzes them into total inaction.

  If you do not have an emergency fund, take heart. You can still create one. Begin by setting a goal that you feel confident you can reach with moderate effort. When that goal has been reached, increase the goal, perhaps to an amount that is one and a half to two times the original goal. Since the ultimate goal is to have sufficient funds in savings to help you weather any emergency, only you can decide how much you need in order to sleep well at night.

- **A Large Purchase**—in years gone by, no one thought twice about buying on credit. It was easy, perhaps too easy, to simply pull out a credit card and buy whatever the heart desired. By saving money until you can pay cash for what you want, you make it easier to live within your means. Consider this: how much easier would it be to pay your weekly bills if you paid cash for a car and did not have to make a monthly car payment? Now, consider *this:* do you think you might be able to negotiate a better price when buying a new car if the sales rep didn't have to wonder if you could qualify for financing? With cash, you have the negotiating power of saying, "Financing is not an issue. The real issue is if you (the sales rep) can come up with a price I'm willing to pay."

- **The Wholly Account**—you know that some expenses are going to come due at some time; even if it's not monthly, they are still inevitable. This is why everyone needs a savings account that is *wholly dedicated* to these anticipated, inevitable expenses. Cars need new tires, appliances wear out and must be replaced, and bills that are paid once a year arrive in the mail. Planning for these inevitable expenses makes it easy to find the money to pay for them. For example, if I know that I've got to buy new tires for the car every three years, and I know that those new tires are going to cost $540, then I also know that I need to deposit $15 dedicated to tires into my Wholly Account every month.

- **Vacations and Luxury Items**—a vacation should be a time to relax and enjoy life, enjoy the fruits of your labor. Although it is much too easy to spend money you don't have while on vacation, wouldn't it be nice to come home with no worries about how to pay off bills that are the result of spending "plastic money"? Not worrying about paying for a vacation that's over would certainly ease the stress of receiving credit card bills afterward.

- **A House**—in the heady days of the '90s, and early 2000s, houses could be purchased with very little or nothing down. The bursting of the housing bubble, the number of foreclosures pending, and the number of vacant foreclosure houses has meant that lenders are much more likely to demand that buyers have "cash in the game," so to speak. Having cash in the game has a real advantage to the buyer. When the home buyer makes a 20 percent down payment, there is no requirement to buy Private Mortgage Insurance (PMI), an insurance policy designed to protect the lender against default. To consider how much PMI adds to your monthly mortgage payment, consider this example.

*Ron and Hollie purchased a house, financing 95 percent of the $150,000 purchase price. Since their credit scores are between 680 and 719, they will pay $111.63 each month for the PMI policy that was required by the lender. Had their credit scores been below 680, the PMI would have cost even more!*

Think about what they could have done with that money if they did not have to pay for PMI.

- **Retirement**—we will discuss retirement more fully in Chapter 11. For now, suffice it to say that most people look forward to the day when they stop working and start enjoying their later years in comfort. To do this, prior planning is essential. That planning means saving money for retirement.

- **Higher Education**—everyone wants the very best for their children: the best home life, the best education, the best future. Studies show that having a degree or certification beyond a high school diploma is key to opening the doors to a better career and a higher income. Although student loans offer a resource to pay for that education, they also are a heavy burden that lasts for years after graduation. Wouldn't it be great for children to come out of school debt free? Saving now for a child's future education can make that dream a reality.

*It is very important to bear in mind that retirement savings should not be sacrificed to pay for college.* You can borrow to pay for college, but you can't borrow to pay for retirement.

## How Do I Save?

As with the reasons to save, there are probably just as many ways to put money aside as there are people offering suggestions. Here are a few to consider.

**Payroll Deductions**—it's hard to miss money if you've never seen it. Having money deducted from your paycheck and deposited into a savings account is a very good way to make savings happen. Just as important as having the deducted funds deposited into savings is having the self-discipline to leave it there. Payroll deductions can be used for emergency funds, the Wholly Account, vacation savings, retirement, and more.

**Automatic Transfers from Checking to Savings Accounts**—do you have a specific goal that you are saving for? How soon do you want to want to reach that goal? Consider this example:

> Cecilia wants to purchase a big-screen television as a surprise gift to her family. Her goal is to pay cash for it and have it set up in time for her husband to watch the holiday bowl games. She has done her homework and found the set that she wants, a 52-inch LED/LCD high definition set that sells for $1,350. Since the holidays are ten months away, Cecilia has $135 transferred from her checking account to her savings account on the first day of each month. In ten months, she will be able to use these funds to pay cash for the television and enjoy the games with her husband—without a worry about how to pay for it when each month's credit card statement arrives!

**Change in a Jar**—at the end of the day, what happens to the change you received when you made purchases? The old phrase "it's just pocket change" is misleading. Those coins really add up! Try this experiment for just thirty days. At the end of each day, deposit all of your coins in a jar. Then—don't touch them. At the end of the month, count the change. How much did you end up with? Now, imagine that you do this every month for a year, a decade, a lifetime. How much money could you accumulate in savings?

Now, put on your thinking cap and you'll probably come up with a few more ways that you can add to this list.

## Where Do I Put My Savings?

Grandma, or maybe it was great-grandma, often talked about keeping money in the sugar bowl or in a coffee can. This allowed her to have a bit of cash right at hand if she came face-to-face with an emergency. Today, keeping enough money in the sugar bowl to deal with an unexpected event would require an awfully big sugar bowl. So where do we keep the savings we need?

The simplest answer is that we keep the money in our local bank or credit union. Let's take a moment here to examine the differences between banks and credit unions.

**Banks** are for-profit financial institutions owned by their shareholders (stockholders). They offer a number of services that include, but are not limited to, checking and savings accounts, safe deposit boxes, certificates of deposit, credit cards, ATM cards, mortgages, and consumer loans. People who place their money in bank accounts are protected against loss due to bank failure by the Federal Deposit Insurance Corporation (FDIC). The FDIC insures deposits up to $250,000.

**Credit Unions** are not-for-profit financial institutions that are owned by, and operated for the benefit of, their members. Like banks, they offer checking and savings accounts, safe deposit boxes, certificates of deposit, credit cards, ATM cards, mortgages, and consumer loans. Money deposited in a credit union is insured against loss due to failure of the institution by the National Credit Union Share Insurance Fund (NCUSIF) for up to $250,000.

As you can see, banks and credit unions have much in common. So what differentiates them?

**Ownership**—while banks are owned by stockholders, credit unions are owned by their members. Bank policies and the board of directors are established at annual meetings attended by the stockholders, who benefit from the successful operation of the bank. People who have money in accounts at the bank have the right to attend annual meetings, but they do not have any voting rights.

Credit unions have no stockholders, so it is the members, the people who have money on deposit in the institution, who benefit from the successful operation of the credit union. Members of the credit union elect the credit union's board of directors at the annual meeting; and the members have the power to determine policy by voting those board members on or off. Only those who have joined the credit union by depositing money into accounts are allowed to vote at the annual meeting or be on the board of directors.

**Fees**—fees are often charged by both types of institution for services such as checking accounts and overdrafts on checking accounts. However, in general, "credit unions charge lower fees and loan rates than banks and pay higher savings yields."[1]

We will repeat this information and cover it in more depth in Chapter 4.

## Conclusion

In this chapter, we learned that saving money is an important part of every household budget or spending plan. But it will not happen unless it is a priority item in that plan.

---

[1] Stephen Brobeck, executive director of the Consumer Federation of America, quoted by Bob Trebilcock on CBS's Moneywatch.com, January 12, 2010.

Knowing *why* we are saving money provides the motivation to save. There are nearly as many reasons to save as there are people who save. Their reasons include

- Planning for occasional emergencies, large purchases, vacations, luxuries, and other periodic expenses

- Ensuring that a child can afford a higher education, that a home can be purchased, or that retirement is not a dream but is a reality that can be enjoyed

People find ways to save. They may

- Have money deducted from each paycheck and deposited into a savings account or retirement plan

- Have their bank or credit union automatically transfer funds from a checking account into a savings account

- Simply throw all of their change into a jar at the end of the day

Finally, we saw that there are differences between banks and credit unions. Banks are for-profit and operate for the benefit of their stockholders. Credit unions are not-for-profit and operate for the benefit of their members. Knowing what makes one place better suited to meeting your needs makes it possible to choose the financial institution that is best for *you*.

CHAPTER 3

# Managing Payroll Deductions

*Bringing Home As Much of Your Paycheck As You Possibly Can*

"Anyone may arrange his affairs so that his taxes shall be as low as possible; he is not bound to choose that pattern which best pays the treasury. There is not even a patriotic duty to increase one's taxes. Over and over again the Courts have said that there is nothing sinister in so arranging affairs as to keep taxes as low as possible. Everyone does it, rich and poor alike and all do right, for nobody owes any public duty to pay more than the law demands."

— Judge Learned Hand
Judge of United States Court of Appeals for the Second Circuit
1924-1961

Think back a few years. It's your first payday. You know how many hours you worked and you know how much you're being paid per hour. You know how much that check should be for, right down to the penny. You can't wait to get your hands on it so you can go do all the things you've been dreaming about. Then you receive the check and can't believe your eyes. Anyone who's ever had a job and can see your face knows

25

exactly what is wrong. You've just gotten your first dose of adult reality. Your paycheck has been pillaged.

Let's take a minute to examine the money that is taken out of gross pay and that determines your actual spendable income. You will find that some deductions are controllable while others are fixed and cannot be changed.

## Federal Income Tax

The first thing you see is that money was taken out for federal income taxes. It may seem that income taxes are completely out of your control, but there are some things you can do to manage how much of this actually comes out of your check.

When planning for income taxes, the name of the game is "don't owe money at the end of the year." For this reason, most people have too much money taken out of their check on every payday. When they get the refund check, they brag about how much money they got back as though it's manna from heaven. The problem, of course, is that it's not a gift; it's actually their own money.

Think of it this way. Let's say you have a favorite banker who invites you to come down to the bank and open a new savings account. He explains that it is a great account: you put one hundred dollars into the account every month for twelve months, and at the end of the year, you can ask for your money. Your favorite banker assures you that he'll be happy to send it to you—in a few months. Oh, and by the way, not one penny of interest will be paid! Ask yourself, "How quickly will I run down to the bank and open this savings account?"

"I wouldn't do it," you say. Why not? Because you have to wait for your own money and you're not being paid a cent for allowing someone else to use your money all year.

So now, consider this: if you will not do this for your favorite banker, why are you willing—happy, in fact—to do it for your "favorite uncle"?

Although there are advisors who will make promises about how large a refund they can help you get, your true goal should be to make the refund check on the inside of the envelope smaller than the postage stamp on the outside of the envelope—in other words, only a small amount of your money was not available to you all year long. How do you attain this goal? By making proper use of the exemptions that determine the percentage of each check that is withheld for federal income taxes.

In order to figure out the proper number of exemptions to claim on the Form W-4 that is submitted to your employer, you can either consult a tax professional, such as a certified public accountant or an enrolled agent, or use the calculator provided by the Internal Revenue Service at its website http://www.irs.gov.

When the calculator shows the proper number of exemptions to claim, complete a new W-4 and submit it to the payroll department at work. In a few weeks, you will see more money in your paycheck. This is money you can use to pay bills, pay off debts, or begin planning for long-term financial goals.

## Earned Income Tax Credits (EITC)

Before moving on to other payroll deductions that can/will be taken from gross income, let's address the subject of earned income tax credits. The Earned Income Tax Credit (EITC) is a tax credit given to individuals who are employed at low wages in order to reduce the amount of income tax that is owed or results in a tax refund. If a taxpayer is receiving earned income tax credits, he or she will often receive a very large tax refund at year end. When this occurs, the wage earner has two choices, both of which can significantly increase take-home pay.

One option is to simply adjust the number of exemptions claimed on the W-4 form to reduce or eliminate any withholding for federal income taxes.

The other option is to file a request with your employer to actually receive the EITC in monthly installments throughout the year as part of your payroll checks.

Among the requirements to receive Advance EITC, an individual must have a valid Social Security Number, be between the ages of twenty-five and sixty-five, have a qualifying child that lives with him or her for at least one half of the year, and cannot file his or her federal tax return as Married, Filing Separately. If you believe that you may qualify for this Advance EITC, consult IRS Publication 596 and complete the worksheet that determines eligibility. If you are eligible, file a Form W-5 with your employer.

## Social Security Tax

The next deduction to come out of the paycheck is for social security taxes. While the income tax withholding is one that we have some control over, the deduction for social security has been established by law: 6.2 percent of every dollar is paid into the social security trust fund.[2] On some pay stubs, the deduction will appear as "Social Security" and on others as "OASDI," Old Age Survivors and Disability Insurance. On still other pay stubs, it will appear as "FICA," Federal Insurance Contributors Act. Regardless of what it is called, it is the same tax and it funds the entire Social Security System. Created by Congress in 1935, the system was designed to provide several benefits.

First, it provides an old age pension for retirees. The age for retirement was originally set at 65 years. At that time, the life expectancy was 58.1

---

[2] For tax years 2011-2012, the employee's payroll deduction for social security taxes was reduced to 4.2% of the gross income in an effort to stimulate the economy by increasing "spendable" income. This reduction has been terminated.

years for an American male and 61.6 years for an American female. A great many individuals were originally excluded from coverage, such as agriculture and domestic workers, railroad workers, government employees, nurses, hospital employees, social workers, and many teachers. The law was subsequently amended to include many of those previously excluded and to provide that an eligible citizen could begin collecting retirement benefits at age 62. However, benefits would be reduced for each year of age collecting benefits before 65. In addition, those citizens who had previously been excluded would be allowed to participate in the program. Today, the age for full retirement benefits is dependent upon the year in which a person was born; that is, a person born between 1943 and 1954 can receive full social security retirement benefits at age 66. But, a person born in 1959 must have attained the age of 66 years and 10 months to receive full retirement benefits.

Second, the Social Security System provides survivors' benefits. In the event of a bread winner's death, the beneficiaries would receive a monthly income based on the benefits he or she had accrued during employment. For example,

> Beth is 35 years old and has two children, Brian, age eight, and Linda, age six. Her husband recently died in an automobile accident and was fully insured under the social security program (this coverage begins when a worker has worked for forty insured quarters). Consequently, Beth will receive a monthly check from the social security system until Brian turns eighteen or graduates from high school, whichever is later. At that time the benefit check that Beth receives will be reduced by the amount that was Brian's share of the benefits; and she will continue to receive the benefits to which Linda is entitled until Linda turns eighteen or graduates from high school, whichever is later. When Linda's benefits terminate, Beth will no longer receive a check from social security and will not be eligible for benefits until she is sixty-two years of age. The years between the termination of the last child's

*social security benefits and the time when the widow
again becomes eligible for survivor's benefits is often referred to as the "blackout period."[3]*

A widow or widower age 65 or older with no children can also receive survivor's benefits.

*Rose, age 70, recently lost her spouse following a short
illness. Both she and her husband were receiving social
security retirement benefits. Rose cannot continue to receive both checks from social security, but she can elect
to receive her husband's benefit payment if it is greater
than the amount that she was receiving.*

Third, the program provides disability income benefits for those who are unable to work due to accident, injury, or illness. To be considered disabled, the worker must have a physical or mental condition that prohibits performing any "substantial gainful activity." In other words, the worker is unable to perform any kind of work. The condition must be expected to last for at least one year or until the person dies from the condition, the worker must be under age sixty-five when the disability begins, and the person must have worked at least five years out of the previous ten years.

Finally, the program provides a death benefit of $255 to defray burial expenses, an amount that has not changed since the inception of the program.

---

[3] There is a number of factors that determine the age at which a child ceases to receive social security benefits following the death of a parent. Contact the Social Security Administration for additional details.

## Medicare Tax

Prior to 1965, a large number of senior citizens had little or no health insurance. The Medicare program was passed to ensure that most seniors would be able to access medical coverage.

Part A pays for hospital care, skilled nursing facility care, and home health care. Hospice care was added to Part A in 1983.

Part B pays for outpatient care, physician's care, laboratory and x-ray services, medical equipment used at home, and home health care costs not covered by Part A.

Part D pays for prescription medications. Part D must be selected when a person first becomes eligible for Medicare in order to avoid a costly penalty fee for joining later. If a citizen has prescription drug coverage through an employer's health insurance plan, enrollment in Part D can be delayed until the employer's coverage terminates. Part D enrollment must then be completed within 60 days of that termination. When a person has Part D coverage, he or she receives a "membership" card that limits the patient's out-of-pocket cost to a co-pay or a deductible. Some Part D plans provide coverage up to a specific dollar amount. Then the patient is responsible for the full cost of the prescription medication until a specific amount has been paid out of pocket. When that maximum expense has been paid, Part D resumes covering the medication again with only a small out-of-pocket co-pay or deductible. This gap in coverage has often been referred to as "the donut hole." Provided by private insurance companies that have been approved by Medicare, Part D can be a part of either a traditional Medicare plan, or it can be part of a Medicare Advantage Plan.

Part C, also known as Medicare Advantage, combines coverages from Part A and Part B. The difference between Medicare and Medicare Advantage is that with the former private insurers that have been approved by Medicare provide the insurance protection, often at lower cost. Part C programs can be administered as health maintenance organizations, preferred provider networks, private fee for service organizations, special needs plans, or a high deductible plan combined with a medical savings account.

The Medicare tax is fixed by law. Currently it is set at 1.45 percent of every paycheck. It should be noted that beginning in January 2014, individuals earning more than $200,000 and families earning more than $250,000 started paying an additional 0.9% Medicare surtax.

Both the employee and the employer pay social security and Medicare taxes in equal amounts. It is worth noting that if a person is self-employed, he or she must pay both the employee's tax and the employer's tax.

## State Income Tax

As of this writing, with the exception of nine states (Alaska, Florida, Nevada, New Hampshire, South Dakota, Tennessee, Texas, Washington, and Wyoming), citizens are subject to state income taxes and money must be withheld from their paychecks to pay this tax.

## Employee Benefits

Employers often offer benefits to their employees. In many cases, the employer has paid a significant portion of the cost of these benefits, leaving only a small amount for the employee to pay. These benefits can include the following:

**Group Life Insurance** can be a straightforward, fixed amount, for example, $10,000. Alternatively, it may be offered as a multiple of the employee's annual salary: one year's salary, two years' salary, or more. The employer may pay all or part of the premium, and all employees who desire coverage will receive it regardless of health or pre-existing conditions. Because group life insurance must cover all who request it, the premiums must take into account the fact that those who have health conditions which might otherwise preclude them from obtaining life insurance are more likely to request the insurance than those who are perfectly healthy. The perfectly healthy may believe that they have no need for life insurance; or they may find that they can obtain the same amount of protection for less money by personally purchasing the insurance outside of the group.

You should be aware of two cautions regarding group life insurance.

First, in years gone by, many individuals spent their entire working lives with the same employer. Having all insurance and retirement plans provided by the employer seemed be quite logical. However, in today's work environment, it is not uncommon for individuals to change employers a few, and perhaps many, times. When this is the case, it is quite common for the employee to lose all benefits including the life insurance provided by the employer.

In a few cases, the life insurance might be convertible from group coverage to an individual policy. This policy would be issued with the normal premiums for a person of that age. In most cases, however, the group life insurance is terminated when employment ends. If the employee has developed a health condition that may shorten life expectancy, he or she may have to pay higher premiums, or may not be able to obtain life insurance at any price. For this reason it is prudent to personally purchase life insurance that the individual owns and controls and that is not dependent on working for a specific employer.

Second, if the employer is paying all or part of the life insurance premiums, the cost of the first $50,000 of insurance does not create a tax liability for the employee. However, under certain circumstances (and those circumstances are *very* common), the cost of insurance that is above the first $50,000 can be deemed to be imputed income on which the employee will owe income taxes, social security taxes, and Medicare taxes. An employee who is insured for more than $50,000 under the group life insurance policy would be well advised to talk with a tax professional who has a professionally recognized competence regarding the Internal Revenue Code, such as a CPA or an Enrolled Agent, to determine if he or she must pay taxes on this imputed income.

**Group Health Insurance**, which will be discussed at length in Chapter 10, may be the most affordably priced health insurance an employee can buy. As with group life insurance, health coverage may be terminated at the end of employment. The Consolidated Omnibus Budget Reconciliation Act (known as COBRA) requires that the (former) employee be given the opportunity to continue coverage for up to eighteen months. However, the full premiums must be paid by the (now) former employee, and, if he or she is unemployed, the premiums may be unaffordable.

**Group Disability Insurance** may be offered to replace lost income when an individual is hurt or sick and unable to work for an extended period of time. The coverage may provide income for a short term (frequently up to 6 six months), a long term (which often begins after 6 months of injury or illness), or both. We will discuss disability insurance in greater detail in Chapter 9. While the group policy *may* be the most cost effective way to obtain this vital protection, it is important to remember that the person who is in excellent health may be able to obtain it at a lower cost by purchasing an individual policy.

**Long-Term Care Insurance** is coverage that pays for hospice care, extended nursing home care, and home health care when a person is unable to perform a number of the tasks of daily living without assistance even though a skilled nursing facility is not needed. While it is typically purchased privately by individuals as they approach age 60, or in the years shortly thereafter, this product has become increasingly popular as an employer sponsored group benefit. The reason is that as employers have sought new ways to recruit and retain outstanding employees. If this program is offered as an employee benefit, the most important question to ask will be "Is the policy convertible to an individual policy if I leave the employer, the group?" If the policy is not convertible, the employee must consider his or her age, the number of years before retirement, and if the coverage continues after retirement. Protection against the costs of extended nursing home care is too critical to invest large sums of money in a policy that will not be available to provide benefits in the (perhaps former) employee's senior years, the time when it is most likely to be needed.

## Qualified Retirement Plans

The traditional pension plan paid a retirement benefit based on the number of years someone worked for an employer. Unfortunately many employers no longer offer this type of retirement plan. Instead of assuming the responsibility for providing a comfortable lifestyle in the employee's "golden years," more and more employers are adopting plans that require the employee to take the initiative of setting money aside, investing it for growth, and accepting the responsibility for how those funds are invested as well as the risk of loss if those investments do not perform well. There are several very common plans that we will briefly explore here.

**401(k)** plans allow the employee to have money deducted from gross pay, usually expressed as a percentage of the gross amount. The employee selects investments from a list of available investment options and directs how much should be placed in the chosen investments. As we will see in Chapter 11, these plans are generally designed for employees of large for-profit companies.

**403(b)** plans operate in a very similar manner, but they are designed for the employees of some 501(c)(3) non-profit organizations, for people who work in cooperative hospital service organizations, and for people who work in public school systems that have elected to offer such plans.

**457** plans also operate in a very similar manner, but they are designed specifically for those who work for state or local governments and some 501(c)(3) organizations.

**Simplified Employee Pension (SEP) Plans, Simplified Employee Pension—Salary Reductions (SAR-SEP) Plans,** and **Simple-IRA Plans** are similar plans that are designed either for small businesses or for those who are self-employed.

The numbers used in the titles of some of these plans simply designate the section of the Internal Revenue Code that permits this specific type plan.

These company sponsored retirement plans provide a great opportunity to chart out life's "golden years." As we will see when we discuss retirement plans in Chapter 11, these plans offer tremendous opportunities to prepare for retirement. However, they also carry restrictions that can make it very expensive to remove funds prior to retirement age. While some employers will match your contribution in some measure, others will not. Do not allow the absence of an employer match to stop you from putting money into these plans. The opportunity to shelter the growth of these funds from taxation is much too valuable to not participate.

## Flexible Spending Accounts

Many employers offer their employees flexible spending accounts that enable the worker to pay certain types of expenses with "before tax" dollars.

There are two kinds of **Flexible Spending Accounts** available to an employee. A **Healthcare Spending Account** (HSA) allows an employee to have money deducted from each paycheck *before* the money is taxed. This money is then used to pay the employee's out-of-pocket medical and dental expenses such as co-pays and deductibles. These funds can also be used for medical and dental expenses incurred by the employee's spouse and dependent children.

The advantage of the HSA is that these accounts enable employees to pay for qualifying medical or dental expenses with *untaxed* money. To appreciate that advantage, consider this example. Let's assume that the employee pays 20 percent of his or her income as federal income taxes.

In essence, twenty cents of every dollar paid from the HSA is money that would otherwise have been paid to the IRS.

Similarly, a **Dependent Care Spending Account** (DCS) allows the employee to pay dependent care expenses with untaxed funds. However, these expenses must be specific, qualifying expenses. One example of a qualifying expense is for child care while the employee is at work. In this example, the child must be under the age of thirteen; or, if over age thirteen, the child must be incapable of self-care due to either physical or mental incapacity. Another example of a qualifying expense is adult day care for senior dependents who live with the employee; that is, parents and grandparents.

When establishing a Flexible Healthcare Spending Account or Dependent Care Spending Account, it is very important to remember that the funds in these accounts are "use it or lose it" money. If these funds are not expended during the calendar year in which they are withheld, the money is forfeited.[4]

## Other Tax Credits

In addition to the Earned Income Tax Credits described above, several other tax credits are available to wage earners that provide the potential to increase the worker's after-tax income.

The **Child Tax Credit** reduces a taxpayer's tax liability when the "qualifying child" is under age seventeen at the end of the tax year; is the son, daughter, step-son, step-daughter; is the descendent of a son, daughter, step-son, or step-daughter; or, is an eligible foster child; or can be claimed as a dependent on the taxpayer's federal tax return. In a small

---

[4] Flexible Healthcare Spending Accounts (FHSAs) should not be confused with Medical Savings Accounts (MSAs). The money in an FHSA should be spent before the end of the calendar year as only a minimal amount can be carried forward from one year to the next; the unspent funds in an MSA, which is tied to a health insurance plan with a high deductible, can be fully carried forward from one year to the next.

number of instances, the credit may exceed the tax liability, in which case, the taxpayer receives a refund that is called an "additional child tax credit." The available refund/credit is dependent on a number of factors and the taxpayer is well advised to consult IRS Publication 972, IRS Form 8812, and a competent tax professional. This tax credit is available only to families whose income is below $130,000.

Because a number of dependent care expenses, such as babysitting and daycare, are not tax deductible, the **Child Care & Dependent Care Tax Credit** was created to help offset (to some degree) those expenses when the costs exceed the income of the second wage earner in a household where both spouses are employed. Because this tax credit is highly variable and dependent on many different factors, consult IRS Publication 503 to determine eligibility.

The American Opportunity Credit, Hope Credit, and Lifetime Learning Credit are all **Education Credits** designed to help offset the costs of education and vocational training. The taxpayer must be saving for or paying the costs of educating a qualifying student at a college, university, vocational/technical school, or other post secondary education institution. IRS Publication 970 provides detailed information about each of these tax credit programs, including eligibility, qualifying expenses, and the differences between the three programs.

Finally, **Retirement Savings Contributions Tax Credits** allow low-income individuals and couples to receive credits against their tax liability for contributions made to qualified retirement plans such as 401(k)s, 403(b)s, IRAs, SIMPLE IRAs, and ROTH-IRAs. There are limitations on adjusted gross income (AGI) that will determine the taxpayer's eligibility for this credit. In order to realize these benefits, the taxpayer must complete and submit IRS Form 8880 with the income tax return.

## CONCLUSION

Taxes mean that payroll deductions to pay those taxes are inevitable. However, the amount withheld for may be controllable.

- Federal income taxes can be controlled by the number of exemptions claimed on the W-4 form filed with your employer.

- The Earned Income Tax Credit (EITC) is a tax credit given to individuals who are employed at low wages.

- Taxes withheld to pay for Medicare and Social Security are fixed by law and cannot be controlled.

- The majority of the states have a state income tax.

Employers often provide benefits as a way to attract top-notch employee candidates and to reward employees for service.

- An employee may have the opportunity to select the benefits that will provide the greatest value to his or her family; choose wisely to make the best use of this opportunity.

- Due to the many types of businesses that employ individuals, the Internal Revenue Code authorizes different types of retirement plans. While these plans may have significant differences, they are all designed to help people plan for their "golden years."

- Flexible Spending Accounts make it possible for the employee to pay certain expenses with untaxed money. But these accounts carry the caveat that they must be used in full each year or leftover funds are forfeited.

Finally, there are numerous tax credits for which people may be eligible. Some will increase take-home pay while others will reduce tax liabilities. In either event, the recipient has more spendable dollars with which to pay for both the "gotta-have-its" and the "wanna-have-its" in life.

## CHAPTER 4

# Establishing a Banking Relationship

*It Pays to Know People with Money*

"In the old days a man who saved money was a miser; nowadays he's a wonder."
Author Unknown

First, a definition of "bank": as used here, a bank is a financial institution that allows you to keep money in a safe place where it is available for use when you need it. Using this definition allows us to include not only banks but also credit unions, both of which fit the definition of a financial institution.

Let's review some of the facts about banks and credit unions that we discussed in Chapter 2.

**Banks** are "for-profit" financial institutions owned by their shareholders (stockholders). They offer a number of services that include, but are not limited to, checking accounts (also known as demand accounts) and savings accounts, safe deposit boxes, certificates of deposit, credit cards, debit cards, ATM cards, mortgages, and consumer loans. People who place their money in bank accounts are protected against loss due to bank failure by the Federal Deposit Insurance Corporation (FDIC). The FDIC insures deposits up to $250,000.

**Credit Unions** are not-for-profit financial institutions that are owned by, and operated for the benefit of, their members. Like banks, they offer checking and savings accounts, safe deposit boxes, certificates of deposit, credit cards, ATM cards, mortgages, and consumer loans. Money deposited in a credit union is insured against loss due to failure of the institution by the National Credit Union Share Insurance Fund (NCUSIF) for up to $250,000.

**What Differentiates Them**

- Ownership—banks are owned by stockholders. Bank policies and the board of directors are established at annual meetings attended by the stockholders, who benefit from the successful operation of the bank. People who have money in accounts at the bank, the depositors, have the right to attend annual meetings, but they do not have any voting rights.

  Credit unions have no stock holders; they are owned by their members; that is, their depositors. So it is the members who benefit from the successful operation of the credit union. Members of the credit union, the people who have their money on deposit in the institution, elect the credit union's board of directors at the annual meeting; consequently, the members have the power to determine the policies of the credit union by voting those board members on or off. Only those who have joined the credit union by depositing money into accounts are allowed to vote at the annual meeting or be on the board of directors.

- Fees—fees are often charged by both types of institution for services such as checking accounts and overdrafts on checking accounts. However, in general, "credit unions charge lower fees and loan rates than banks and pay higher savings yields."[5]

## What Services You Will Need

Deciding what kinds of services you need when you establish your banking relationship will require a bit of thought and planning. Consider these questions:

- Do I receive a sum of money at the beginning of the month or semester that I have to manage over a period of time?

- Where do I want to keep my money until I need it?

- What expenses will I need to pay?

Many students, for example, receive a lump sum of money in the form of student loans, grants, or funds from home at the beginning of each semester. This money must be rationed out to pay expenses throughout the semester.

The first thought regarding where to store funds until they are needed is to keep the money close by, in our wallets or in our homes so that we can get it whenever we feel the need. However, this strategy has several flaws. Wallets get lost. Homes get robbed. Money stored in the sugar bowl finds its voice and calls out to us, seducing the unwary into spending money on wants rather than holding on to it for later needs.

The expenses that must be paid often should guide the selection of banking services that best meet the needs of the depositor. So, let's take a look at some of the available services.

---

[5] Stephen Brobeck, executive director of the Consumer Federation of America, quoted by Bob Trebilcock on CBS's Moneywatch.com, January 12, 2010.

## Checking Accounts

Checking accounts are often referred to as "demand accounts"; in other words, the funds are available to you when you request them. For example, your monthly rent is due on the first day of each month. Rather than taking cash to the landlord, you can write a check that the landlord then deposits into his or her account. The landlord's financial institution presents your check to your bank or credit union which then transfers the appropriate amount of money from your account to the landlord's account.

If you do not have as much (or more) money in your account as the check is written for, your bank will return it to the landlord's bank stating that you have insufficient funds. Your bank will charge you an overdraft fee, and the landlord may also charge an "NSF" (non sufficient funds) fee. These fees will significantly increase the cost of the transaction.

Years ago people wrote checks before the money was actually in their accounts, knowing that the money would be deposited on the next day or the day after that. This was known as "playing the float"—the person writing the check was counting on the need for a few days to process the paperwork before the check got back to the bank demanding the transfer of the money. Today checks are processed almost instantaneously, and the funds really need to be in the account when the check is written. In fact, some merchants have machines right at the register that process the check and ask your bank to transfer the funds immediately.

Checking accounts frequently offer the convenience of debit cards. While the card may have a credit-card-like logo on it, it is significantly different from a credit card. Use of this card *immediately* transfers money from your checking account into the account of the store or facility where you use it. Although these cards are very convenient, it is important, first, to make sure that there is enough money in the account when it is used, and, second, to record the transaction just as you would when a check is written to make sure you do not overdraw your account and incur the fees referred to above.

When you open a checking account, the bank or credit union will ask for personal information including your name, address, telephone number, and social security number. This enables the institution to contact you regarding your account and to provide information regarding any interest, which is taxable income, the account may earn during the year.

One final note regarding checking accounts is important to keep in mind. Checking accounts frequently have monthly service fees attached to them. The bank or credit union may waive the service fee if a specified minimum amount of money is kept in the account at *all* times. If you have this type of account, it is important to make sure your balance never goes below the minimum balance requirement. Should the balance go under the minimum at any time, the monthly service fees will be collected.

## How to Write a Check

A check is simply a piece of paper that authorizes your financial institution to transfer money from your account into someone else's possession. Let's take a look at a blank check.

| | | |
|---|---|---|
| John X. Smith | | 1001 |
| 123 Oak Street | Date _____ | |
| Anytown, Florida 30000 | | |
| | | |
| Pay to the Order of: _____ | $ _____ | |
| _____ Dollars | | |
| | | |
| Memo _____ | _____ | |
| 000000000 : 12345678901234 : 1001 | | |

In the top left corner are the name and address of the account holder. The top right corner shows the check number that is used to record the check in the check register.

On the "Pay to the Order of" line, you write the name of the person or business to which the money is to be paid; in this case, the "Sack of Grub Grocery Store."

---

John X. Smith                                                    1001

123 Oak Street                           Date __May 15, 2011__

Anytown, Florida 30000

Pay to the Order of: __Sack of Grub Grocery Store__    $ _____

_____ Dollars

Memo _____      _____

000000000 : 12345678901234 : 1001

---

John X. Smith                                                    1001

123 Oak Street                           Date __May 15, 2011__

Anytown, Florida 30000

Pay to the Order of: __Sack of Grub Grocery Store__    $ _105.39_

_____ Dollars

Memo _____      _____

000000000 : 12345678901234 : 1001

---

On the line next to the dollar sign, you write in the amount of money to be paid. Let's say, $105.39.

To ensure that no one can alter the amount of the check and obtain more money than you intended to pay, on the next line spell out the amount of money that was indicated next to the dollar sign. The memo line is used for record keeping to indicate what the check was written for. In this case, the check was used to purchase food and household supplies.

Finally, the person writing the check signs his or her name on the line to the right of the memo line.

When you have done all this, the check will look like this.

| | |
|---|---|
| John X. Smith | 1001 |
| 123 Oak Street | Date _May 15, 2011_ |
| Anytown, Florida 30000 | |
| Pay to the Order of: _Sack of Grub Grocery Store_ | $ _105.39_ |
| ---- _One Hundred and five and 39/100_ ---- | Dollars |
| Memo _Food & Household Supplies_ | _John X. Smith_ |
| 000000000 : 12345678901234 : 1001 | |

Those numbers at the bottom of the check are magnetically encoded and tell the financial institution's computer about the account the money is coming from.

| | |
|---|---|
| John X. Smith | 1001 |
| 123 Oak Street | Date _____ |
| Anytown, Florida 30000 | |
| Pay to the Order of: _____ | $ _____ |
| _____ | Dollars |
| Memo _____ | _____ |
| 000000000 : 12345678901234 : 1001 | |

The first nine numbers, indicated within the brackets above, are the bank's routing number, an electronic address.

47

John X. Smith                                                  1001

123 Oak Street                        Date _____

Anytown, Florida 30000

Pay to the Order of: _____ $ _____

_____ Dollars

Memo _____      _____

000000000 : 12345678901234 : 1001

The next group of numbers is the account number, again indicated by the brackets, from which the money is to be withdrawn. This number is John X. Smith's account number. The combination of the routing number and the account number ensures that the funds are transferred out of John's account and not from the account of someone else.

The last four numbers match the check number. This allows the check to be processed by the computer so that it appears on John's monthly account statement.

**Balancing Your Checking Account**

Once each month, you will receive your account statement. Delivered either on paper or electronically, the statement shows all your checks processed by your bank during the month. It also allows you to determine which checks have not been processed yet. To see how to balance the check book, let's look at the example below.

*Mauricio wrote three checks in January and five checks in February. The checks were*

*#315—on January 1, to Three Fountains Apartment Gardens, $500. The statement he received in February showed that his bank processed the check on January 4.*

*#316—on January 19, to the Bread & Butter Grocery Store, $127.39. The statement he received in February showed that his bank processed the check on January 21.*

*#317—on January 29, to Your Electric Company, $121.54. This check did not appear on the statement he received in February.*

*#318—on February 2, to Three Fountains Apartment Gardens, $500.*

*#319—on February 5, to the Bread & Butter Grocery Store, $47.98.*

*#320—on February 18, to Acme Auto Parts, $14.72.*

*#321—on February 21, to the Bread & Butter Grocery Store, $44.99.*

*#322—on February 28, to Your Electric Company, $133.75*

Today is March 4 and Mauricio has received his new statement. The statement is shown below.

| Opening Balance | | $645.98 |
|---|---|---|
| #317 | Feb. 3 | (121.54) |
| Deposit | Feb. 4 | 157.99 |
| #318 | Feb. 6 | (500.00) |
| #319 | Feb. 9 | (47.98) |
| Deposit | Feb. 12 | 214.17 |
| Deposit | Feb 19 | 212.88 |
| #321 | Feb 25 | (44.99) |
| Deposit | Feb 26 | 289.99 |
| Closing Balance | | $806.50 |

The statement shows the date on which each check (shown in parentheses) was processed, and each deposit (shown without parentheses) was processed.

Seeing the closing balance, Mauricio's first thought is that he has a lot more money in the account than he thought he did and maybe he can take his girlfriend out to a fancy dinner. But as he reviews the statement, he sees that the check to Acme Auto Parts ($14.72) and the check to Your Electric Company ($133.75) have not yet been processed (a process often referred to as "clearing the bank"). To determine how much money he really has available, he must subtract these outstanding checks from the closing balance.

$$\begin{array}{r} \$\,806.50 \\ -\,14.72 \\ -\,133.75 \\ \hline \$\,658.03 \end{array}$$

After doing the math, Mauricio sees that he has $658.03 available. In addition he knows that he paid his $500 rent on March 2. Consequently, he actually has only $158.03 that he can spend.

Writing down each check as it is written (also called "recording it in the check register") is a good way to make sure you never overdraw your account. And remember, using the debit card is the same as writing a check.

## Savings Accounts

A savings account is just what it says it is, an account in which money is saved for a future need. The bank or credit union pays interest on the account. This money can be lent by the bank to other consumers to buy houses, cars, and other items that are too expensive for them to pay cash for. In essence, the institution is paying you interest for the use of your money to loan to others, and then in turn collect interest from the others on the loan.

Savings accounts are a great place to store money for emergencies. The money is available when you need it, and the bank pays you for storing it there.

## Safe Deposit Boxes

A safe deposit box is a drawer, usually a small one, inside the vault at the bank or credit union. Boxes are rented for a specific period of time, for example a year, and important papers and other valuables can be stored in the box for safe keeping.

## Certificates of Deposit

Like a savings account, a certificate of deposit (also known as a CD) is an account in which money is stored for future use. It typically pays a higher interest rate than a savings account because the depositor promises not to withdraw the money for a specific period of time. For example,

> *Lucinda has received a gift of $500 from her grandmother so that she can pay for text books next fall. Since she knows she will need the money in September and because she wants to make sure she does not spend it before then, she takes it to her bank and deposits it into a certificate of deposit that matures on the last day of August.*
>
> *Because Lucinda has promised to leave the money in the account until the end of August, the bank has agreed to pay her 3 percent interest on the CD rather than the 2 percent interest it would pay on a regular savings account.*

When a certificate of deposit matures, the account owner has the choice of moving the money to another account or of purchasing a new CD.

## Credit Cards

Credit cards are simply a line of credit issued by your bank that allow you to spend money that you do not currently possess. Typically, these cards carry a logo that indicates the credit card network which they are a part of, such as Visa or MasterCard. Because these are unsecured loans, they usually charge higher interest rates than those charged on a loan that is secured by real property, like a car loan.

## Debit Cards

Unlike credit cards that allow you to spend money that you do not have, debit cards are linked directly to your checking account and withdraw funds from that account each time you use it. If you spend more money than you have in the account, the bank will charge you an overdraft fee just as if you had written a paper check when you had insufficient funds.

## Mortgages

A mortgage loan is a loan that enables people to purchase a house. This is an example of a secured loan in that it uses the house as collateral. If the borrower fails to make payments on the loan, the bank or credit union will repossess the house through a process known as foreclosure.

## Consumer Loans

Consumer loans are loans that allow people to borrow money for the purchase of a consumer item such as a car, refrigerator, washer, or dryer. Like mortgage loans, they are secured by the goods that are purchased with the funds. If you fail to make the car payment, the car will be repossessed.

## Other Bank Services

Banks and credit unions frequently offer services in addition to the checking accounts, savings accounts, safe deposit boxes, certificates of deposit, credit cards, debit cards, mortgages, and consumer loans described above. Here is a short list of other services that might be offered.

- Direct Deposit—many employers will deposit paychecks directly into the employee's personal checking account. Some banks and credit unions will either waive or reduce monthly service fees when the account holder signs up for direct deposit.

- On-Line Banking—it is often possible to access your checking and savings accounts from your computer. Here, you can pay bills; review account statements; balance your checkbook; and see which checks, if any, have not yet cleared. Some financial institutions offer this service for free; others charge a fee. Be sure to consider the fees that will apply to you when choosing your bank or credit union.

- Telephone Banking—this service allows you to check account balances, transfer money from one account to another; stop payment on a check; and report lost, stolen, or damaged credit cards or debit cards.

- ATM Banking—automated teller machines allow you to conduct normal banking transactions such as making deposits and withdrawing cash, even if the bank or credit union is closed. These transactions are often performed using your debit card.

- Pre-Paid Cards—these cards, also known as "stored value" cards, are "loaded" with a set amount of money that the user can then use to make purchases. Whenever the card is used, the amount of the purchase is deducted from the funds that were entered onto the card.

## Who's Who at the Bank

There are some key people you really want to get to know at your bank or credit union. They can help make your banking experience enjoyable.

- The first person you will meet when you open your account is the **Customer Service Representative**. This person will explain the services that are available, provide written information about banking products, and refer you to other employees who specialize in certain functions.

- Whenever you go to the bank or credit union to make a deposit or withdrawal (whether you walk in or go to the drive-through window), you will work with a **Teller**.

- If you want to borrow money, the **Loan Officer** will help you fill out your application, provide a written explanation of different loan products, and answer any questions that you may have.

- The **Branch Manager** manages all of the institution's operations in that specific branch. This is the person who can usually help when other employees can't.

## Conclusion

The term bank as used in this chapter refers to two types of financial institutions that provide a wide variety of financial services.

- For-profit, commercial banks are owned by stockholders and operated for the financial gain of those stockholders.

- Not-for-profit credit unions are owned by the members, those individuals who have opened accounts and deposited funds. Credit unions are operated for the benefit of their members.

The services offered by these institutions include

- Checking Accounts make it possible to transfer funds from your account to someone else by filling in the blanks on a check and signing it. Money can also be taken from your account and paid to someone else when you use a debit card.

- Savings Accounts enable you to store money for use at some future time. These accounts pay interest to the owner of the account.

- Safe Deposit Boxes allow you to store important documents in a drawer inside the institution's vault.

- Certificates of Deposit, frequently referred to as "CDs," are similar to savings accounts in that they store funds for future use. They differ from savings accounts in that the depositor promises to leave the funds in the account for a specific period of time. In exchange for this promise, the depositor receives a higher rate of interest than is offered on a savings account.

- Credit Cards are unsecured lines of credit issued by the bank or credit union that can be used for the purchase of goods and services when a person may not currently have the funds to pay for them. They are frequently part of a larger network such as Visa or MasterCard.

- Debit Cards withdraw money directly from your checking account in the same manner as writing a paper check. They are often linked to an ATM card.

- Mortgage loans are loans used for the purchase of a house and use the house as collateral on the loan.

- Consumer loans are loans used to purchase consumer goods such as cars and refrigerators. The goods purchased with the loan typically serve as collateral on the loan.

- Direct Deposit permits you to have money, for example, your paycheck, deposited into your account without your receiving a check and having to go to the bank to make a deposit yourself.

- On-Line Banking and Telephone Banking enable you to access your account via telephone or computer.

- Pre-paid gift cards (stored-value cards) are "loaded" with a set amount of money that the user can then use to make purchases.

The key employees you want to know at your bank are the

- Customer service representative

- Teller

- Loan officer

- Branch manager

It's important to balance your checking account on a regular basis, usually each month, to ensure that you do not write checks that are returned for insufficient funds (NSF) and incur the fees that are charged when this happens.

## Chapter 5

# HOUSING, TRANSPORTATION, AND UTILITIES

*Home—Where We Live, How We Get There, and What We Use There*

"It takes hands to build a house, but only hearts can build a home."

— Author Unknown

As we begin to build our budget, specific expenses must top the list of essential items. One of life's essentials is shelter. Another is household utilities: water, power, and gas. In our mobile society, transportation is another essential. Let's look at these items and the costs that are associated with them.

## Housing

No matter where you live, be it the smallest cottage or the finest castle, it is your home. It is safe refuge from a troubling and sometimes hostile world. To ensure that you always have a "roof over your head," housing is considered the priority expense. In other words, of all your expenses, it must be the first thing planned and accounted for.

If a person owns his or her own home, the monthly mortgage payment is only one of many necessary and recurring expenses. In addition, the following items must be on the list of housing expenses.

- **Property Taxes**—every locality collects property taxes. These taxes usually pay for local schools, public libraries, street and sidewalk maintenance, emergency services (like police, fire, and ambulance coverage), and the costs of administering the municipality or the county in which you live. That's a lot of benefits that would be hard to live without. Property taxes are adjusted over time as home values fluctuate and the costs of tax-financed services escalate. Many property owners have one-twelfth of the annual property taxes added to their monthly mortgage payments. These funds are held in an escrow account and then paid directly to the taxing district by the mortgage holder.

- **Homeowners Insurance**—any homeowner who has a mortgage can be certain that the lender will insist that the structure be insured. This insurance policy will protect both the homeowner and the lender against losses due to fire and other perils that can destroy the building. The homeowner also enjoys protection against theft, loss of use, liability, and much more. We will explore this insurance in depth in Chapter 6. Just as with property taxes, many homeowners have one-twelfth of the annual insurance premium added to the monthly mortgage payments and held in an escrow account so that the funds will be available when the policy renewal premiums are due.

- **Home Maintenance**—in order to maintain the home's value and livability, regular maintenance must be performed. The most obvious maintenance expense is grounds keeping. This includes not only water for the lawn, but also fertilizers, equipment (like lawn mowers and edgers), and pest control. Some people perform all of these tasks themselves while others hire someone to do them. Of course, the building also must be maintained with painting, caulking, and roofing. When something indoors breaks, like a water heater, furnace, or air conditioner, it is the homeowner who is responsible for getting the necessary repairs from a competent professional and paying for those services, whether in a home or a condominium.

- **Homeowners Association Dues**—if the residence is located in a planned unit development or is part of a condominium development, the local association will assess monthly or annual fees for the maintenance of common areas such as entry landscaping, clubhouses, recreation areas, swimming pools, and gym facilities. The amount of the dues will depend on the size of the development and the amenities provided by the association. It is common to have these dues kept in an escrow account.

Renters have typically felt that they were immune to all of these expenses. After all, the landlord has to paint when necessary and is responsible for cutting the grass and weeding the flower beds. And when something in the apartment or home breaks, a call to the landlord should be all that is needed to make everything right. The wise consumer, though, recognizes that the landlord plans to obtain the funds for these fixes from one source: the tenants. Landlords include the costs of these maintenance expenses, along with construction costs or purchase price and property taxes, in determining the rent charged to the tenants.

## Transportation

Getting from "Point A" to "Point B" sounds easy enough. Simply get in the car and go! But where did the car come from? Is it owned? Or perhaps it's leased. Then again, maybe you don't have a car at all and instead take public transportation. Whatever the means, transportation costs must be included in the budget.

Let's begin by assuming that a vehicle is going to be purchased. The first thing to decide is whether it will be new or used. Either way, few people have the ability to pay cash for the car, so it must be financed. This, then, is a logical starting point.

**Financing** the purchase of an automobile is a serious matter and should not be left to chance. A wise consumer will shop around and determine not only who offers financing, but also what the prevailing interest rates are on auto loans. While many dealerships offer to help the buyer obtain financing, they may not be the best places to get the loan. Instead, you should begin by talking with the loan officer at your own bank or credit union. Determine if pre-approval is possible. When the loan is pre-approved, the buyer is able to approach the seller with the confidence that financing is not an issue; only the price is. In addition this approach limits the number of inquiries submitted to credit bureaus during the process. Remember, each hard inquiry lowers your credit score, which then has the impact of raising the interest rate that will be charged on the loan.

One other factor should be considered. In the past, auto loans were limited to two- or three-year durations. Today these loans can run for four, five, six years and longer. A known strategy of auto salesmen is to ask what monthly payment the buyer wants to pay. When the buyer commits to a specific monthly payment, he or she pays less attention to the actual cost of the car and tends to focus on the fact that the payment is "affordable." Let's assume for a moment that John and Mary are two consumers, each shopping for a new car. Both have chosen the same make and model car. John wants the lowest monthly payment possible and does not consider the long-term effect of extended monthly payments. Mary, on the other hand, recognizes that fewer monthly payments will save her money over the long term.

*Mary's Loan*

*Loan Amount = $15,000*

*Loan Interest Rate = 6.00%*

*Monthly Payment = $352.28*

*Mary's forty-eight payments ($352.28 x 48) will total $16,909.44.*

*John's Loan*

*Loan Amount = $15,000*

*Loan Interest Rate = 6.00%*

*Monthly Payment = $248.59*

*John's seventy-two monthly payments ($248.59 x 72) will total $17,898.48.*

While John's loan appears to be the better deal because he has a lower monthly payment, Mary will pay $989.04 less for her car! The numbers demonstrate which financing package is better.

There are several other factors to consider in order to get the best price on a new car.

- Do your homework in advance. Fortunately, the Internet has made it much easier to do this research, a subject that we'll pursue further in a moment.

- Determine the best time to go shopping. Believe it or not, there are some times that are better than others. For example, at the end of the month, salespeople are often eager to make a sale so that they can meet their quota.

- Look at the sticker inside the driver's side door that tells the date the car was manufactured. The longer the car has been on the lot, the better the chance of negotiating the price down. The interest on the dealer's floor plan financing continues to accrue and costs the dealer money while the car sits on the sales lot.

- Compare different nameplates. Some companies have the same basic model under different brand names. The vehicles share the same frame, body style, and even features, but one is less expensive than the other solely because of the brand on the nameplate.

To ensure that you get the best price on a used car, there are also several factors to consider.

- Get an idea what the car is actually worth. Websites such as the Kelly Blue Book (www.kbb.com), the NADA Guide (www.nada-guides.com), and Edmunds (www.edmunds.com) all provide the ability to research both new and used cars. Some websites also offer reviews of the vehicles.

- Use the car's vehicle identification number (VIN) to check (1) the car's history to determine if it has been involved in an accident or suffered some type of damage such as from flooding, (2) if there are discrepancies in the car's mileage versus the odometer setting, and (3) if the car has a salvage or junked record. Vehicle histories are available at sites such as Carfax and AutoCheck.

- Check the car's safety record at the National Highway Traffic Safety Administration's website (www.nhtsa.gov) to see how well it withstands crashes and how well it protects the driver and passengers.

- Finally, shop around for great buying opportunities. Some car rental companies sell their fleet vehicles when they have reached a specific number of miles. The car has been well maintained and often carries the manufacturer's original warranty up to the years and mileage limits. Name brand car dealers will usually get first pick of trade-ins and off-lease vehicles. If the dealer has taken a model of its own brand in trade, the car may be sold as a "certified" car carrying a manufacturer's warranty. Non-dealer car lots often obtain their cars at the auctions or from other dealers. One final note: there are some dealers who prey on individuals who have encountered hard times. They offer credit to those who can obtain credit nowhere else at interest rates that border on usury. Think twice when what you can get seems too good to be true.

## Fuel

As a country song says, cars don't run on faith. For the most part, they require either gasoline or diesel fuel. Each person's fuel requirements are dependent on distances traveled, the number of trips driven each day or week, and the mileage delivered by the car's engine (not to mention "lead-foot syndrome"). This is another area where tracking your personal fuel spending patterns enables you to better anticipate how much money must be set aside in your monthly budget.

## Vehicle Maintenance

Many people think of maintenance as strictly oil changes and lube jobs. However, there are some other expenses that should be planned in advance. For example, tires must be replaced when the tread is worn down to the indicator bars. To be sure that new tires can be purchased when they are needed, set money aside each month toward the cost of replacements. If your tires cost $600 and you must replace them every two years, divide the $600 cost by 24 months and save $24 each month so that you can pay cash when the time comes. Do the same thing for brakes, batteries, fan belts, and routine maintenance like oil changes and lube jobs.

## Other Expenses

License plates, as mentioned earlier, must be renewed, in most cases, every year or two. Once again, money can be set aside each month to reserve the funds needed for this expense.

If you use toll roads, money should be budgeted for the tolls. Unlike the lady in the first chapter who just assumed that the toll fairy put money into the box thingie on the windshield whenever it was needed, we know that we must plan for this recurring expense.

## Utilities

Utilities are a matter of prioritization. There are no good utilities and bad utilities. There are only needed utilities and wanted utilities.

### Needed Utilities

**Water,** as we noted earlier, is definitely one of the "gotta-have-its" of life. Without water, we die. However, individual bottles of water aren't necessities. For those who like to carry bottles of water wherever they go, why not purchase a reusable bottle and refill it as necessary? This not only saves money, it also reduces the amount of trash dumped into landfills every day.

Unless we want to live like our nineteenth-century ancestors, **electricity** is another essential utility. Everything in our homes from the lights and heating and air conditioning to the hot water in the shower to the refrigeration that keeps our food from spoiling depends on a steady supply of electric power. In homes that rely on water drawn from a well, electricity usually powers the pumps that draw the water from the ground.

As mentioned earlier, many electric companies now offer levelized billing plans that help consumers plan for the monthly power bill. In this type of plan, the electric company adds the last twelve months of electric bills together and then divides by twelve to determine an "average" bill. The consumer pays this amount each month until the average is reset. Resets can occur once a year, twice a year, or every three months. To illustrate,

*Ryan and Amy use electricity for all the power needs in their home. The table below illustrates their electric bills for the past twelve months.*

| | |
|---|---|
| January | $200.00 |
| February | $180.00 |
| March | $100.00 |
| April | $105.00 |
| May | $115.00 |
| June | $150.00 |
| July | $200.00 |
| August | $200.00 |
| September | $120.00 |
| October | $130.00 |
| November | $150.00 |
| December | $200.00 |
| | |
| Total | $1,850.00 |
| Divide by 12 | |
| Monthly Average | $154.17 |

Beginning in January, Ryan and Amy will pay $154.00 each month until the next adjustment date. Now, assume the following usage, dropping off the first three months from above and adding the next three months at the end.

| | |
|---|---|
| April | $105.00 |
| May | $115.00 |
| June | $150.00 |
| July | $200.00 |
| August | $200.00 |
| September | $120.00 |
| October | $130.00 |
| November | $150.00 |
| December | $200.00 |
| January | $250.00 |
| February | $225.00 |
| March | $195.00 |
| | |
| Total | $2,040.00 |
| Divide by 12 | |
| Monthly Average | $170.00 |

*Beginning in April, Ryan and Amy will pay $170 each month until the next adjustment date, probably at the end of June.*

In some months they will pay more than their actual usage for the month would cost. However, in other months they will pay less than the cost of their actual power usage. The advantage of this levelized billing is that it enables them to *plan* for the bills for the next three months. And after all, the whole purpose of our budget is to plan how our money will be used.

**Natural Gas and/or Propane** are frequently used to power home furnaces, water heaters, and clothes dryers. When gas is a power source, in some months the electric bills will be lower, and in other months the gas bills will be lower. It's important to plan for these bills just as we plan for electric bills. Consider the couple below.

*Jose and Carla heat their home with propane. The propane tank must be filled twice a year, once in October and once in February. The semi-annual cost to fill the tank is $240.00, so it's $480.00 a year for propane. In order to pay for these refills, Jose and Carla will need to save $40.00 each month so that the funds are available to pay for the gas each time the tank is filled.*

All of these utilities—**water, electricity, and natural gas/propane**—are "gotta-have-its." Although we must have and plan for them, we can still find ways to save money on them. For example, we can turn off lights when leaving a room, and turn thermostats down in the winter and up in the summer. Wise consumers identify ways to save that are compatible with their lifestyles, and then implement those strategies.

Unless we haul or burn our own trash, we rely on a **garbage collection** service to haul it away for us. In many locations, the cost of this service is simply added to another utility bill such as the water bill; in others it may be included in the annual property taxes. Whatever the schedule for payment, the funding to cover it should be included in the monthly budget.

## Discretionary Utilities

If there has ever been an area where the difference between the "gotta-have-its" and the "wanna-have-its" has gotten blurred, discretionary utilities are a great example. The "gotta-have-its" are those things that are basic to life. "Wanna-have-its," on the other hand, are those things that are surely nice to have, but life *really* does not end without them. Consider the following.

**Cable/Satellite Television** is definitely nice to have. The convenience and variety of having hundreds of channels to choose from is wonderful, but, as hard as this may be to accept, they really are luxuries. The extinction of the human race is not imminent if we forego them. For someone living in a rural area where conventional television reception is poor or non-existent, a case can be made for basic cable service in order to stay connected to the world, but declining the luxury packages of additional channels is a smart money saver.

Purchasing both **hard-wired telephone service in the house and cell phone service** is not always necessary. The expansion of cell service to rural areas empowers a consumer to decide if both are truly *essential*. Some will choose cellular service in order to have access to emergency services when traveling. Others will decide that the only telephone they need is the one in the house. Some "phone" companies offer packages that include television and Internet. The variety of options enables consumers to purchase the service that best meets their *needs*.

One final note regarding the costs of telephone service. As a financial counselor, I have actually been told by clients that they need not worry about long distance charges because they use pre-paid long distance cards. Inasmuch as these cards do not grow on long distance card trees, the wise consumer will determine how long a card lasts and how much is required to "refill" the card. Then, money can be reserved each month to refill or purchase a new card as needed.

Touching again on the "gotta-have-it" vs. "wanna-have-it" question, one opinion that's becoming increasingly difficult to dispute is that **Internet access** is a necessity in today's world. On-line news providers bring us information from all over the world. Employers are increasingly requiring applicants to submit resumes and applications for employment electronically. Voice over Internet Protocols (VoIP) and video over Internet providers make it possible for people to communicate with business associates, friends, and loved ones over the Internet rather than making long distance phone calls. Often these VOIP providers offer low cost or no cost service. Customers can face bewildering packages of Internet service bundles that cost less—or more—than the purchase of individual services. The savvy consumer should closely examine the services offered to determine what is truly *needed* and what is just a luxury that is not essential to life.

**Alarm systems** can provide peace of mind and a sense of security. Two options are available: monitored and unmonitored. When triggered, monitored systems alert emergency services. Knowing that law enforcement, fire fighters, or emergency medical help is on the way offers reassurance that we are not at the mercy of forces beyond our control. Unmonitored alarm systems merely make noise in the hope that neighbors will alert emergency services. If you are contemplating the purchase of an alarm system, determine what is needed in your circumstances and what is not.

## CONCLUSION

Housing, transportation, and utility costs are often among the largest expenses we face and are definitely the highest priorities we must plan for. Some of these are essential "gotta-have-its" while others "nice-to-have-its."

Housing is clearly an essential, but the cost of housing does not stop at the house payment itself. Housing expenses include

- Property taxes

- Property insurance

- Property maintenance

- Association dues

On first glance, renters may believe that they are exempt from these costs, but, in reality, these expenses are built into the rent calculation.

In a mobile society, transportation costs are another essential and include

- Cost of vehicle and payments

- Fuel

- Auto maintenance

- License plates

- Fees for using toll roads

In some locales, public transportation may be chosen in lieu of these expenses. In others, they may be in addition to these costs.

Utilities may be either essential expenses or discretionary expenses. The essential "gotta-have-its" include

- Water

- Electricity

- Natural gas and/or propane

While the items above are "gotta-have-its," discretionary utilities provide us with an opportunity to pick and choose what we buy since it is possible to live without

- Cable and satellite television with premium channels

- Hard-wired telephones AND cell phones

- Alarm systems

Recognizing the difference between wants and true needs enables us to obtain the best values for our dollars and to have the things that we truly *do need*.

## CHAPTER 6

# Fine Dining on a Budget

*Let's Eat!*

"They take great pride in making their dinner cost much; I take my pride in making my dinner cost so little."

— Henry David Thoreau

Some people eat to live. Others live to eat. Whichever group you belong to, one thing is certain. For most families, food is a major expense, typically second in line after shelter. The key to eating well on a budget is planning meals in advance and ensuring that each meal includes the proper nutritional components to build and maintain healthy bodies.

The first step is to *plan* meals ahead of time. Several years ago, I provided financial counseling for a lady who shared her smart budget strategy for grocery shopping. Every week she plans her meals and makes a list of the ingredients she needs to prepare those meals. She then checks her pantry and crosses off the items that she already has. Then she finds coupons and items on sale. At the store, she buys only what's on her list, and nothing else.

Clearly, she has a plan and works it; and it works for her.

Another approach could save even more money. Check the ads and coupons first. Then plan the menus for the week around whatever is most cost-effective.

Whichever method you choose, having it all worked out in advance empowers you to stay focused at the grocery store and to avoid impulse buying.

Another practice that can get you the best value for your grocery store dollar is to buy in bulk whenever possible and practical. Stores often sell family packs in the meat department and family size cans in the canned good department. Many consumers buy in bulk and repackage in smaller portions at home.

In addition, some stores run sales in cycles. By identifying and taking advantage of them, you can coordinate meals far in advance. For example, your local market may put chicken on sale during the first week of every month. Recognizing this, you can buy chicken not just for this week's meals but for meals in the coming weeks, too. This helps save money—as well as provide convenience—if you can make room in the freezer to store the extra chicken until it is needed.

Similar concepts—using coupons and buying in bulk—also apply to non-edibles like paper goods, laundry products, and cleaning supplies. Toilet tissue sold in multi-roll packages typically has a lower per roll price than buying only a two-roll package. The jumbo box of laundry detergent usually has a lower per ounce cost than the same amount in smaller boxes. (See the section on breakfast cereals below.) Many of the money saving coupons you see are for these products.

Speaking of coupons, in a 2009 article on its website, consumeraffairs. com stated that an average of *$318 billion* worth of grocery coupons were issued in 2008 and that only *$3 billion* worth were redeemed.[6] Everyone knows the usual sources of coupons: newspapers, magazines, and store flyers. But other sources include websites such as

- www.couponmom.com

- www.hotcouponworld.com

- www.coupons.com

- www.thegrocerygame.com

- www.befrugal.com

While there are other websites, clients and others have strongly recommended these five over the past several years.

Another great place to get coupons is coupon exchange groups you can form with family, friends, and neighbors. Many of the people you know use coupons that you don't use; and you use coupons that they don't use. Why not exchange coupons with these folks so that everyone benefits?

Finally, a smart household money manager finds ways to get great value at low prices. Cleaning supplies can often be purchased inexpensively at discount stores where nothing is priced over $1. However, be cautious at these stores. In some instances, they may be selling a product that has been packaged in a smaller than usual container so that it can be sold at a "bargain" price. When the per unit (per ounce) cost is compared to larger packages sold elsewhere, the "bargain" is no longer a good deal.

---

[6] ConsumerAffairs.com, April 19, 2009.

As you probably know, every store has a plan to help you spend *more* when you shop. For example,

- Most stores place higher priced items at eye level. Think about the breakfast cereal aisle. The name brand cereals are on the shelves at eye level. Generic cereals and lower priced bulk packages will either be on the top shelves or on the lowest shelves. Keep in mind the adage that, for most products, the least expensive items "live up high and down low."

- Note where the more expensive prepared (frozen) foods are in the stores where you shop. Begin your meal planning and shopping with items that are in the other areas of the store—fresh fruit, fresh vegetables, dairy products, breads, and less expensive cuts of meat. Buy the prepared foods only when necessary.

- Higher priced "impulse" items are often displayed at the checkout counter to entice you while you wait your turn. Put on your blinders and resist the temptations.

- Stores often use some advertised items as "loss leaders," products that they are willing to sell at or below cost in order to entice shoppers into the store with the expectation that they will then purchase the remainder of their groceries at prices that provide the store with a comfortable profit. It's a good idea to remember that sales are held for a purpose (to get the customer in the store) and that you may be able to get the greatest value for your grocery dollar by shopping at a second store in order to take advantage of each store's advertised specials. (Note: Rather than saving money, shopping at too many stores will burn extra gas and time.)

- Many stores advertise that they have "everyday low prices." In some cases, they do, in fact, offer the best bargains on many products. In other situations, advertised and unadvertised sale items will offer a better value. For this reason try to keep track of the cost of items that you purchase regularly so that a real bargain can be distinguished from a bargain that really isn't.

- Pre-cut produce is usually sold with the enticement of convenience. However, you can save a lot of money by doing your own peeling and chopping at home.

- Meat products offer several different ways to save money. Check the "sell by" date on the package. If today is the "sell by" date, ask the butcher or meat department attendant to mark the price down. Many stores will honor this request because they don't want to throw the product away at the end of the day. If they won't mark the product down at that time, ask what time of day they *do* mark these packages down and make it a point to shop at that time in the future. Another way to save money on meats is to buy inexpensive cuts that tend to be less tender. You can ask the butcher to run them through their tenderizer, or you can cook them in a crock pot or at a low temperature for a longer period of time. Slow cooking at low temperatures will make nearly any cut of meat "fork tender." Examples of these lower priced cuts include chuck roasts, chuck steaks, and briskets.

Here are a few more ideas of how to save money at various meals.

- **Breakfast**

    o Check the unit prices for cereals. While bulk packages will usually cost less per ounce, manufacturers know that consumers think that bigger is always cheaper. Sometimes the smaller box will sport a lower cost per ounce than the family size package—not always, but sometimes.

    o Avoid individual size packages of instant hot cereals such as oatmeal, cream of wheat, and grits; make the real thing. It takes just a marginally longer time and not only is it less expensive but evidence suggests that it may be more healthful. For variety, try adding spices such as cinnamon, cloves, and allspice to oatmeal. Or add dried fruits such as raisins, cranberries, mixed fruits, pineapple, mango, etc. to the oatmeal to create a variety of flavors. If you have leftover pieces of sausage or bacon, chop them up and add them to grits for a change of pace.

o Check bakery outlets (they were once known as "day-old stores") for reduced prices on breakfast staples such as fruit and cereal bars, breakfast breads, pastries, and English muffins.

o Remember that eggs are an inexpensive breakfast food and can be prepared in a wide variety of ways.

o When serving bacon at breakfast, cut the strips in half. Family members will still feel like they've had a specific number of bacon strips, but in reality have consumed half as many, thereby saving on food laden with cholesterol as well as on costs laden with fat.

- **Lunch**

o Instead of buying pre-packaged sliced lunch meats (like ham or turkey), buy a boneless ham or turkey breast and ask a butcher to shave it. Shaved slices on bread give the appearance of a thicker sandwich.

o When packing sack lunches, pack foods that will actually be eaten rather than thrown away by finicky eaters.

o Avoid pre-packaged lunch trays of meat, cheese, and crackers. Instead, assemble your own lunch tray. The lunch you create will be far less expensive, and healthier.

o   When adding chips to the lunch, package a portion of chips in a snack size plastic bag rather than buying individual serving sized bags.

- **Dinner**

  o   Stock up on proteins such as meats, fish, and poultry when they are on sale, and freeze for future use. Be sure to properly package these foods prior to freezing to guard against freezer burn.

  o   Plan at least one "meatless" meal each week.

  o   Stretch meats by letting them be the accent to a dish rather than the main course. For example, add some diced ham or sliced smoked sausage to a pot of green beans and potatoes; or create a chicken and rice casserole that contains more rice than chicken.

  o   Some meats such as hams and turkeys will typically go on sale before major holidays, making that a good time to stock up on these foods. After holiday meals, divide leftovers into meal-size portions and freeze for convenient use later.

  o   Soups can be a great lunch or dinner. Make your own by using leftover meat, bones, and vegetable trimmings to make your own soup stock.

    - Beef stock can be used to make a vegetable soup of a beef and barley soup.

    - Add vegetables and noodles to a chicken or turkey stock.

    - Ham bones can be boiled to make a stock that forms the basis for a bean or split pea soup.

With any of these stocks, store them overnight in the refrigerator before making your soups. All of the fat and grease will rise to the surface and solidify. You can then remove the solid fats to create a low fat, low cost, healthy, and very tasty meal.

There are many, many great resources for additional information on economical meal ideas. Here are a few to get you started.

- www.foodnetwork.com (one of my personal favorites)

- www.allrecipes.com

- www.myrecipes.com

- www.campbellskitchen.com/recipes

- www.pillsbury.com/recipes

- www.recipesecrets.com

- www.bhg.com/recipes

- www.food.com

- www.foodreference.com/html/recipes.html

Finally, take any leftover food at the end of the meal and store it in airtight containers in the refrigerator. Once a week, have "leftover night" where the objective is to turn the leftovers into a great meal at low or no cost. Be creative—you might surprise yourself and your family with how well it turns out!

## CONCLUSION

Food is another one of life's gotta-have-its.

From a nourishment perspective, making certain that we eat proper quantities of the different food groups ensures that we eat nutritionally balanced meals. Eating right allows us to build and maintain healthy bodies, which in turn may help keep health care costs down.

From a monetary perspective, planning ahead is key to resisting the siren songs of creative grocery marketers who are more concerned with increasing the store's profitability than with adhering to our budgets. Planning right allows us to build and maintain healthy finances.

To ensure that we prevail in the struggle between marketing and budgeting, we must have a plan:

- Use coupons

- Buy what's on sale

- Buy In bulk

- Note store sales cycles

- Use other print and electronic resources

- Purchase non-food goods at dollar-pricing stores

If you are willing to plan ahead, try new things, and experiment a bit, you will find that you and your family are eating better—for less—than you ever thought possible!

Insurance

## CHAPTER 7

# Insuring Your Home and Its Contents

*Renters, Homeowners, and Condominium Insurance*

"He is the happiest, be he king or peasant, who finds peace in his home."
— Johann Wolfgang von Goethe

Whether you live in an apartment, a condo, or a single family home—as a renter or as an owner—protecting your possessions against loss or damage is very important. Obviously, if the worst should happen, you want to be able to replace furniture, clothing, and other valuables. In addition, if you purchase a home, the lender will require property insurance to protect itself should the structure suffer from fire, hurricane, or other events that impact value. The lender does not want to have a pile of ashes collateralizing the loan.

All property insurance policies share some common elements. It's the protection options that differentiate one from another. Let's begin with the typical homeowners insurance policy. Some provisions common in this type of policy are also in renters and condo owners policies, and some provisions are not.

## Homeowners Insurance

**Coverage A—The Dwelling**—this part of the policy insures the building itself. Although there are several different forms of homeowners insurance, the most commonly purchased is Form HO-3, also known as an "all perils" policy. It insures the homeowner against all types of losses except those that are specifically excluded. The specific exclusions are typically

- Earthquake

- Nuclear accident

- Acts of war

- Flood

The last one is often a source of confusion, so let's explain the difference between water damage and flood damage.

**Water Damage** is caused by plumbing leaks and *falling water*. Let's say, for example, that a severe storm causes a tree limb to fall onto the roof and damages it, allowing rain to enter the house. Any losses resulting from the falling water entering the house will be covered.

On the other hand, **Flood Damage** is caused by *rising water*. In the case of the storm above, water rises (perhaps from a river overflowing its banks or just from the street) and enters the house. Any losses resulting from the rising water will not be covered by a homeowners insurance policy.

When a house is damaged by a covered peril, that is, fire, hail, or a tornado, Coverage A pays to repair or rebuild the structure. It will also pay for removing debris from the site and cleaning up the damage. What this means to the property owner is that, when the structure is damaged or destroyed by a covered peril, the insurance company, rather than the homeowner, writes the check that pays for the cleanup and repairs.

Homeowners should be aware of the co-insurance clause in homeowners policies. Because only a small percentage of homes are totally destroyed, it is common for claims against the policy to be for far less than the complete replacement of the structure and its entire contents. Consequently there is a great temptation for some homeowners to save money by insuring their homes for only a portion of the cost to entirely rebuild. For this reason, insurance companies include the co-insurance clause, a requirement that the house be insured for a minimum of 80 percent of the cost of total replacement. If the coverage provided by the policy falls below the required 80 percent, the insurance company deems the homeowner to have chosen to partially self-insure.

To illustrate how this clause will impact the homeowner in the event of a partial loss, consider this example.

> Carl and Patricia own a home that, in the event of total destruction, would cost $100,000 to completely rebuild. However, their insurance policy covers the structure for only $60,000; the home is insured for just 60 percent of any loss. While dinner was being prepared one evening, a grease fire caused $9,000 damage to the kitchen. Because the house is insured for only a 60 percent loss, the insurance company will pay only $5,400 toward the repair of the kitchen. Carl and Patricia will be responsible for the remaining $3,600. In other words, the owners cannot simply collect up to $60,000 worth of damage.

Had Carl and Patricia had the home insured for at least $80,000 (that is, the 80 percent required for full coverage), the entire repair bill would have been paid by the insurance company. Because the cost of rebuilding increases over time due to increased labor and materials costs, it is imperative that the homeowner compare the cost of rebuilding with the coverage provided by Coverage A in the insurance policy. Here's how to determine the cost of rebuilding:

- Determine the total square footage of the house "under roof." If the garage is attached to the house, include it in the square footage. A detached garage is not included in this calculation.

- Contact reputable contractors to determine the cost per square foot to rebuild a house. Explain why you are asking this question so that the contractor will be better able to provide accurate information.

- Multiply the number of square feet by the cost per square foot to find the amount of insurance needed in Coverage A.

Let's use Carl and Patricia's house as an example.

*Carl and Patricia's home has 1,750 square feet. Because the cost of rebuilding when they bought the house was $57.14 per square foot, they needed $100,000 in Coverage A. One year after purchasing the house, they found that the cost of rebuilding had increased to $60.00 per square foot. They needed to contact their insurance company and increase Coverage A based on $105,000 in rebuilding costs.*

As a general rule, most homeowners insurance policies will calculate other coverages such as the amount of money available to rebuild outbuildings or replace the contents of the house as a percentage of Coverage A.

Since a renter in a house, a condo, or an apartment will suffer no loss if the building is destroyed (the renter does not own the building), a renters policy does not include Coverage A.

**Coverage B—Outbuildings**—outbuildings are defined as other structures on the property that are not attached to the house; for example, a detached garage, a storage shed, or a swimming pool enclosure that is not attached to the house. Coverage B pays to repair or rebuild these structures in the event that they are damaged by a covered peril (a cause of damage that the policy protects against). What this means to the homeowner is that rather than his having to pay the cost of repair or replacement "out of pocket," the insurance company will pay these costs.

As a general rule, Coverage B is set at 10 percent of Coverage A. So if Carl and Patricia have $100,000 in Coverage A, their outbuildings will be insured for $10,000.

Since renters do not typically own outbuildings, Coverage B is not included in a renters policy.

**Coverage C—Contents**—the contents of your home include everything in the house: your clothing, furniture, jewelry, electronics, appliances, tools, toys, frozen food, spices. Everything!

Moreover, your personal property includes anything you buy while away from home, too. For example, let's say you are traveling in Switzerland, purchase a cuckoo clock, and have it shipped to your home. If it is lost in transit, Coverage C in your homeowners insurance policy will pay to replace it. It is worth noting here that, if you bought the clock with a credit card, the card might also provide coverage that would replace the clock, helping you avoid making a claim that might later lead to the cancellation of your homeowners policy.

As a general rule, Coverage C is set at 50 percent of Coverage A.

One very important point to keep in mind when discussing Contents Coverage is that some personal property, such as jewelry, firearms, and collectibles, has a limited amount of coverage. If the item is worth more than the limit, it must be scheduled (individually listed along with a professional appraisal of the item's value) in order to be insured for full value. To illustrate, let's revisit Carl and Patricia.

*Carl gave Patricia a very large, flawless, diamond necklace for her birthday. The value of the necklace far exceeded the single item limit of their policy, so they needed to schedule this piece of jewelry for it to be fully insured. Carl had to get a professional appraisal of the necklace's value and have his insurance agent submit the appraisal to the company along with the request that it be specifically identified and fully insured on the schedule.*

Since both owners and renters possess personal property, Coverage C is included in not only homeowners policies, but also in both renters and condo owners policies.

**Coverage D—Loss of Use**—when a home is damaged, it is not uncommon for the damage to be severe enough that the occupant cannot reside in the home while it is being rebuilt or repaired. When this happens, a family will incur expenses that they would have had to pay without this coverage. Let's return to Carl and Patricia's grease fire.

*As a result of the fire damage to the kitchen and smoke damage to the remainder of the house, Carl and Patricia had to live elsewhere while their home underwent repairs. The contractor indicated that he would require three months to repair the house. Furthermore, it took three days for Carl and Patricia to find an apartment that offered a short-term lease. Consequently, they had to rent a hotel room for three nights and eat all of their meals for that time in a restaurant. In addition, because the smoke damage destroyed their sofa, recliner, and bedding beyond salvage, they had to rent furniture for the apartment.*

Let's pause for a moment to determine how these four coverages protected Carl and Patricia following their kitchen fire.

- Coverage A paid to repair all of the physical damage in the kitchen and remediate the smoke and water damage in any other part of the house. It also paid for debris removal.

- Coverage B did not apply because their property included no outbuildings.

- Coverage C paid to replace the home furnishings damaged by the fire, including the kitchen furniture, the living room furnishings, and the bedroom furnishings along with the sheets, pillowcases, blankets, and clothes that were unusable due to smoke damage. It also paid for all of the food that spoiled in the refrigerator and freezer because the power was turned off and all of the unusable food in the cupboards that had to be thrown away after exposure to the high heat of the fire.

- Coverage D paid the hotel bill for the three nights they spent in the hotel, the restaurant meals for those three days, and the furniture rental. In addition, because they had to continue making their home mortgage payment, it also paid the rent on the apartment they lived in.

**Coverage E—Liability**—it's one of every homeowner's greatest fears—that someone will be injured on his or her property. It doesn't matter if the injury is accidental or the result of the homeowner's negligence. The injured party does not want to pay the bills out of his or her own pocket. This is where Coverage E steps up to protect the homeowner. If the medical bills exceed the amount of money provided by Coverage F (which we'll look at next), Coverage E will pay the difference and may also pay for lost income. If the injured person sues the homeowner, it will pay the homeowner's legal fees to defend against the lawsuit. And if the homeowner loses, it will compensate the injured person for damages including actual, punitive, and pain and suffering.

The amount of liability coverage is selected at the time the policy is purchased; for example, $100,000. As a general rule, liability coverage is relatively inexpensive and the consumer should purchase as much as possible.

Inasmuch as a person can be injured in your home regardless if it is owned or rented, Coverage E is included in homeowners, condo owners, and renters insurance policies.

**Coverage F—Medical Expenses**—when a person is injured in your home or on your property, Coverage F pays the individual's doctor and hospital bills.

Again, since a person can be injured in your home or on your property regardless of ownership, Coverage F will be included in homeowners, condo owners, and renters insurance policies.

**Endorsements**—an endorsement is coverage that is added to the standard policy. Here are several endorsements that are strongly recommended.

- **Replacement Cost Coverage**—we talked earlier about Coverage C and how it will replace the damaged contents of the home. The amount of money that will be paid is based on whether the coverage is for the item's "actual cash value" (also known as its depreciated value) or replacement value. Actual cash value coverage reimburses for the purchase of an identical item the same age and in the same condition as the damaged item before it was damaged. Replacement cost coverage pays for a brand new item. Let's see how this applies to Carl and Patricia's refrigerator.

  *You will recall that Carl and Patricia had a ten-year-old seventeen-cubic-foot refrigerator at the time of the fire. Actual cash value coverage would provide enough money to buy another ten-year-old refrigerator of the same size. In essence, they would have to shop at used appliance stores to find one. Replacement cost coverage, on the other hand, made it possible for them to go to their local appliance store and buy a brand new refrigerator of the same size.*

Although replacement cost coverage is more expensive, at the time of need it greatly eases the burden of getting back to normal in terms of time, trouble, and out-of-pocket expenses. Personal property can be damaged or destroyed regardless whether the structure is owned or rented. If financially possible, replacement cost coverage (rather than actual cash value coverage) should be added to a homeowners policy, condo owners policy, or renters policy.

- **Ordinance and Law Coverage**—when a home is built, construction must adhere to the building codes that are in effect at the time of construction, at minimum. However, when a damaged home has to be rebuilt, it must be rebuilt to the codes that are in effect at the time of the rebuild, not the code that existed at the time of original construction. Because building codes are frequently upgraded to include additional safety features, rebuilding frequently costs more than building to the old code would have cost. Let's look at one small part of a rebuilding project.

  *Leon owned a home in South Florida that was built in 1980. When his home was destroyed by Hurricane Andrew in 1992, he was required to rebuild it to the newer, stricter code requiring that every window be impact resistant when a 2" x 4" x 6' board strikes it traveling at 34 miles per hour. The new windows were significantly more expensive than the originals.*

  Because Leon had purchased an Ordinance and Law Endorsement, the higher cost of these windows was paid by the endorsement rather than being taken from Coverage A, a charge which would have left less money to rebuild the remainder of the house. Reconstruction of the entire house was subject to stricter, more expensive requirements, so the endorsement benefited the owner by absorbing the costs of many of the new requirements.

Because a renter does not own the building, the Ordinance and Law Endorsement is not available on a Renters Policy.

- **Flood Insurance**—we noted earlier that a standard homeowners policy does not cover flood damage; neither does a condo owners or renters policy. For damage caused by *rising water* to be covered, the policyholder must purchase a separate policy from the National Flood Insurance Program. Flood insurance, which can be purchased through most property and casualty agents, pays to repair or replace the damage caused by flooding.

- **Earthquake Insurance**—like flood insurance, earthquake protection must be purchased as a separate policy. It is not included in a standard homeowners policy, condo owners, or renters policies. Let me repeat the following for condominium owners.

When most people hear the word "earthquake," they automatically think of the San Andreas Fault line that runs through California. Few think of the New Madrid Fault line located in southern Illinois, western Tennessee and Kentucky, northeast Arkansas, and southeast Missouri. (Fewer still anticipate a quake like the August 2011 one centered in Virginia, which doesn't even lie on an active fault line but is located within the Central Virginia Seismic Zone.) Yet the New Madrid has been every bit as destructive, historically speaking, as the better known San Andreas. For example, four major earthquakes in 1811 and 1812 changed the course of the Mississippi River and destroyed more than 150,000 acres of forest land. At a minimum, those who live in areas that have obvious earthquake risk should seriously consider protecting their assets against loss and contact their property and casualty insurance agent about this type of policy. Those who don't live in those areas might want to consider it, too.

# Condominium Owners Insurance

Many condo owners think that they do not need to purchase condominium owners coverage due to the mistaken belief that the condo association's property insurance will protect them from loss. Unfortunately, this is not the case.

The association most assuredly does have insurance. In the event of a loss, a fire for example, it will rebuild the building from the studs OUT—the exterior of the building only. To rebuild the interior of the building, the owner must own a condominium owners policy. Also known as an HO-6 Policy, condo insurance has most of the same provisions as the homeowners policy.

**Coverage A—The Dwelling**—dwelling coverage rebuilds the interior of the home. Just like its counterpart in a homeowners policy, it repairs or replaces the drywall, the flooring, plumbing, wiring, and fixtures—everything from the studs IN.

**Coverage B—Outbuildings**—this coverage usually does not apply to condominium owners. However, if outbuildings, such as a detached garage, are present, this coverage is needed.

**Coverage C—Contents**—just like Coverage C in a homeowners policy, contents coverage repairs or replaces the contents of the dwelling, paying the depreciated value of an item unless a Replacement Cost Coverage endorsement has been purchased. It insures the owner's personal property (such as clothing, furniture, electronics, etc.).

**Coverage D—Loss of Use**—loss of use coverage pays living expenses when an insured peril causes the owner to seek other housing, and it pays for living expenses, exactly as is done in a homeowners policy.

**Coverage E—Liability**—liability coverage protects the owner in the event that someone is injured within the owner's residence.

**Coverage F—Medical**—finally, as with a homeowners policy, medical coverage pays the medical expenses incurred when a guest is injured while on the owner's premises.

**Endorsements**—an endorsement is coverage that is added to the standard policy. Here are several endorsements that are strongly recommended.

- **Replacement Cost Coverage**—we talked earlier about Coverage C and how it will replace the damaged contents of the home. The amount of money that will be paid is based on whether the coverage is for the item's "actual cash value" (also known as its depreciated value) or replacement value. Actual cash value coverage reimburses for the purchase of an identical item the same age and in the same condition as the damaged item before it was damaged. Replacement cost coverage pays for a brand new item. Let's see how this applies to Carl and Patricia's refrigerator.

  > Carl and Patricia had a ten-year-old seventeen-cubic-foot refrigerator at the time of the fire. Actual cash value coverage would provide enough money to buy another ten-year-old refrigerator of the same size. In essence, they would have to shop at used appliance stores to find one. Replacement cost coverage, on the other hand, made it possible for them to go to their local appliance store and buy a brand new refrigerator of the same size.

  Although replacement cost coverage is more expensive, at the time of need it greatly eases the burden of getting back to normal in terms of time, trouble, and out-of-pocket expenses. Personal property can be damaged or destroyed regardless of whether the structure is owned or rented. If financially possible, replacement cost coverage (rather than actual cash value coverage) should be added to a condo owners policy.

- **Ordinance and Law Coverage**—when a condominium is built, construction must adhere to the building codes that are in effect at the time of construction, at minimum. However, when a damaged condominium has to be rebuilt, it must be rebuilt to the codes that are in effect at the time of the rebuild, not the code that existed at the time of original construction. Because building codes are frequently upgraded to include additional safety features, rebuilding frequently costs more than building to the old code would have cost. Let's look at one small part of a rebuilding project.

  *Jack owned a condominium in South Florida that was built in 1980. When his condominium was destroyed by Hurricane Andrew in 1992, he was required to rebuild it to the newer, stricter code requiring that every window be impact resistant when a 2" x 4" x 6' board strikes it traveling at 34 miles per hour. The new windows were significantly more expensive than the originals.*

  Because Jack had purchased an Ordinance and Law Endorsement, the higher cost of these windows was paid by the endorsement rather than being taken from Coverage A, a charge which would have left less money to rebuild the remainder of the house. Reconstruction of the entire house was subject to stricter, more expensive requirements, so the endorsement benefited the owner by absorbing the costs of many of the new requirements.

  Because a renter does not own the building, the Ordinance and Law Endorsement is not available on a Renters Policy.

- **Flood Insurance**—we noted earlier that a standard homeowners policy does not cover flood damage; neither does a condo owners or renters policy. For damage caused by *rising water* to be covered, the policyholder must purchase a separate policy from the National Flood Insurance Program. Flood insurance, which can be purchased through most property and casualty agents, pays to repair or replace the damage caused by flooding.

- **Earthquake Insurance**—like flood insurance, earthquake protection must be purchased as a separate policy. It is not included in a standard homeowners policy, condo owners, or renters policies. Let me repeat the following for condominium owners.

When most people hear the word "earthquake," they automatically think of the San Andreas Fault line that runs through California. Few think of the New Madrid Fault line located in southern Illinois, western Tennessee and Kentucky, northeast Arkansas, and southeast Missouri. (Fewer still anticipate a quake like the August 2011 one centered in Virginia, which doesn't even lie on an active fault line but is located within the Central Virginia Seismic Zone.) Yet the New Madrid has been every bit as destructive, historically speaking, as the better known San Andreas. For example, four major earthquakes in 1811 and 1812 changed the course of the Mississippi River and destroyed more than 150,000 acres of forest land. At a minimum, those who live in areas that have obvious earthquake risk should seriously consider protecting their assets against loss and contact their property and casualty insurance agent about this type of policy. Those who don't live in those areas might want to consider it, too.

**Extra Loss Assessment**—one endorsement that can be added to a condo policy that is *not* available on a homeowners policy is Extra Loss Assessment. When the condo association's insurance is insufficient to pay for all the damages done to the building, the association has the ability to levy a special assessment in order to obtain the necessary funds to complete the repairs. When this occurs, the condo owner must pay with his or her own funds unless the Extra Loss Assessment Endorsement has been added to the policy. This endorsement pays the assessments with funds from the policy so that the owner need not pay the assessment out of pocket.

## Renters Policies

As is the case in condominium associations, apartment building owners will have an insurance policy that protects them against damage to their building and liability if someone is injured in the building or on the property. And, just as with the condo association's policy, the possessions of the tenant are not covered by this policy. An HO-4, or Renters, Policy insures the tenants against losses.

**Coverages A and B** do not apply to Renters Policies.

**Coverage C—Contents**—contents coverage repairs or replaces the contents of the dwelling, paying the depreciated value of an item unless a Replacement Cost Coverage endorsement has been purchased. It insures the tenant's personal property (such as clothing, furniture, electronics, etc.) just as in a homeowners policy.

**Coverage D—Loss of Use**—loss of use coverage pays living expenses when an insured peril causes the renter to seek other housing, and it pays for living expenses, exactly as it does in a homeowners policy.

**Coverage E—Liability**—liability coverage protects the renter in the event that someone is injured within the renter's residence.

**Coverage F—Medical**—finally, as with a homeowners policy, medical coverage pays the medical expenses incurred when a guest is injured while on the renter's premises.

## What Factors Determine the Premium?

To determine the level of risk incurred when insuring the property, the insurance company will look at a number of factors.

- What is the likelihood of a loss?

- What is the house made of? Brick, concrete block, and wood frame have different insurance implications. The more flammable the building materials, the greater the potential for loss in the event of a fire.

- What kinds of roofing materials were used? Tile, slate, and metal roofs are less likely to burn than fiberglass-asphalt based shingles. And all of these are less likely to burn than shake or wooden roofing.

- How close is the nearest fire station? Proximity to a fire station generally means a shorter response time and less damage to the building in a fire.

- Are there fire hydrants in the neighborhood, and, if so, how close is the nearest one? As with the fire station, the nearness of a water source equates with faster fire control. Interestingly, in many locales, a body of water such as a lake or swimming pool may be substituted for hydrants depending on the volume of the lake or pool.

- What are the crime statistics in the area? Higher crime stats usually mean a greater risk of loss due to burglary, robbery, and vandalism.

- What kinds of claims on this policy have been filed in the past and what was the nature of the claims? Individuals who file a large number or frequent claims may represent an unacceptable level of payouts to companies. Frivolous and/or excessive claims that rise above the actuarial average may cause the company to charge a higher premium, cancel a policy, or even refuse to issue the policy.

- Are there added risk factors?

- Is there a swimming pool on the premises? If so, is there a fence around the yard to keep others away from the pool, or is the pool enclosed by a screen enclosure with lockable doors? By their very nature, pools hold an allure for children who, if they fall into the water, may drown. A pool that is not enclosed in some manner creates a higher risk of liability if it is determined that the homeowner's negligence resulted in injury or death.

- Is there a dog (or other potentially threatening pet) on the premises? If so, what breed of dog is it? Some breeds are considered "high risk" animals. Examples of high risk dogs include pit bulls (also known as Staffordshire terriers), Rottweilers, Siberian huskies, and Chows. Pet owners should talk with their insurance agent about added liability.

## Conclusion

- Property insurance protects our homes against losses, whether the dwelling is a home, condominium, apartment, or duplex, and whether you are an owner or a renter.

- These policies are comprised of different coverages, each designed to protect various parts of the property.

    o Coverage A covers the cost of rebuilding the structure, and a percentage of the amount of coverage here may be used to determine the amounts of other coverages.

    o Coverage B covers the cost of rebuilding structures that are not attached to the house.

- o Coverage C repairs or replaces contents of the specified structures.

- o Coverage D pays the living expenses incurred while the home is being repaired following a loss if the house cannot be lived in.

- o Coverage E provides protection if we are held liable for the injuries someone suffers on our property.

- o Coverage F pays the medical bills for someone who is injured on our property.

- You can get even more protection by purchasing endorsements such as

  - o Replacement cost coverage

  - o Ordinance and law coverage

  - o Flood coverage

  - o Earthquake coverage

  - o Condominium owners may want to purchase an endorsement for Extra Loss Coverage.

Many different factors determine the price of the property insurance policy. By keeping them in mind when choosing where to live, you can ensure that you select the proper coverages and that the cost of protection is not prohibitive.

Insurance

## CHAPTER 8

# Automobile Insurance

*You'll Never Guess Who You Ran into Today...*
*and What It Cost!*

"It takes 8,460 bolts to assemble an automobile and one nut to scatter it all over the road."

— Author Unknown

When we were young, most of us couldn't wait to get our driver's license. Four wheels and the freedom to come and go as we pleased—who could ask for anything more?

Actually state laws could. All fifty states and the District of Columbia require automobile insurance. Each of these entities sets its own requirements about the terms of what drivers *must* purchase. There are many websites that provide an overview of state minimum requirements. One that I have found helpful is http://www.Moneyunder30.com/minimum-auto-insurance-coverage-requirements-by-the-state.

These minimum requirements are just that: minimal requirements that seldom provide the protection that individuals and families truly need in a lawsuit happy world. So let's take a look at the various parts that snap together to form the insurance policy, what each part is, what it does, and what it really means to you, the consumer.

## Liability Coverage

When we first look at an auto insurance policy, one of the first things we see and hear about is a set of numbers; for example, 10/20/10. Like deer caught in the headlights of an oncoming car, many people stare at the numbers, dazed and confused, and wonder what they really mean. These figures indicate the amounts of liability coverage the policy provides. OK, but why are there three different numbers? Why can't it just say, "You're covered for this much"? In fact, it does just that—about the three different kinds of liability.

**Bodily Injury Liability**—this is the part of the policy that pays for the damage that you do to another *person*. It pays for expenses caused by accident related injuries, such as doctor bills and hospital bills. It also pays for damages if someone sues you and wins the lawsuit. The first number tells us how much money will be paid for any one individual, and the second number tells how much money will be paid for all individuals combined.

For example, in the first paragraph, we used the numbers 10/20/10. The first two numbers tell us that the policy will pay up to $10,000 for any one individual to a maximum of $20,000 for all individuals who are hurt in an accident. Let's consider four friends and a careless stranger.

> *Ethan, Frank, Gina, and Helen are riding northbound on Highway 1 in Ethan's new car, a luxury SUV that cost him more than $45,000. Mike, an inattentive driver traveling westbound on Alpha Road, illegally runs through a stop sign, striking Ethan's car broadside on the passenger side*

*of the car. All four individuals in Ethan's car are hurt and require medical treatment.*

*Mike is deemed to be the at fault driver, the one who caused the accident, and receives a citation for failure to obey the stop sign.*

*The medical bills for each individual in Ethan's car are $5,000, or a total of $20,000.*

Since Mike had bodily injury liability coverage in the amount of $10,000 per person to a maximum of $20,000 per accident, all medical bills are paid by the insurance company. But, what if the bills totaled more than $20,000? What if...

*Ethan and Frank were both seated on the driver's side of the car, the side not struck in the collision. Consequently, their injuries were not severe and they had small medical bills, $1,000 each.*

*Gina and Helen, both of whom were on the passenger side of the car, the side struck by Mike, suffered serious injuries and had much higher medical bills. In fact, Gina's treatment cost $35,000, and Helen's hospital bill was more than $100,000.*

*In total, Mike's carelessness caused these four people to incur $137,000 in medical bills.*

Mike now has a problem. His policy will not pay more than $20,000 for the entire accident. Ethan, Frank, Gina, and Helen will have a combined total of $117,000 in medical bills that won't be paid for by Mike's insurance company. Mike can be held responsible for *personally* paying these unpaid bills with his own money.

Purchasing adequate bodily injury coverage could have protected Mike against that personal liability for the bills listed above.

**Property Damage Liability**—this third figure in the three-part number tells us how much the policy pays for the damage that the at fault driver does to the other driver's car. It will either repair or replace the vehicle.

> *In our example above, Mike's insurance policy provided 10/20/10 coverage. The third number in this example tells us that Mike's insurance company will pay to repair Ethan's car; in this case, $10,000.*
>
> *Had this been a minor fender bender, the bill to repair Ethan's car may have been less than $10,000. Unfortunately for Mike, he was traveling at 45 miles per hour and Ethan's car is damaged beyond repair; it is a total loss.*
>
> *Because Mike caused the accident, his insurance company will give Ethan a check for $10,000 to replace his $45,000 car. Since this is not sufficient to replace the vehicle, Mike can be held personally responsible for the additional $35,000 needed to purchase a replacement car for Ethan.*

Interestingly, property damage liability will pay for more than just the repair of another person's car. It also pays to repair or replace the property that was damaged, regardless of whether the property is a tree, a living room wall, or any other piece of property. For example, in the 1991 movie *Doc Hollywood* the main character ran into a new fence that a neighbor had just built. Property damage liability coverage could have paid to repair or replace the fence, though it might not have helped Doc Hollywood given the attitude of the judge.

By any and all measurements, liability coverage is relatively inexpensive and drivers should purchase as much of it as possible. A policy that provides $100,000/$300,000 of bodily injury liability protection costs only marginally more than a policy providing $10,000/$20,000. The price difference between the maximum coverage (the penthouse) offered by the insurance company and the barest minimum coverage (the bargain basement) permitted by the state is usually a matter of only a few dollars a month. Why would anyone settle for the bargain basement when they could live in the penthouse for only a few dollars a month more?

## Personal Injury Protection (PIP)

Also known as no fault coverage in states that use a no fault system, Personal Injury Protection (PIP) pays the medical bills of an injured person regardless of who the at fault driver is.

In addition to paying medical bills after an auto accident, PIP also covers the following costs:

- Replacement of lost wages up to policy limits

- Rehabilitation; psychiatric, physical, and/or occupational therapy

- Funeral expenses, up to the policy limits, when death is the result of an auto related injury

- Medical bills of the injured person even if that person was a pedestrian at the time of the accident

A typical basic PIP endorsement provides $10,000 of coverage per person. If the accident we discussed above had occurred in a state that requires no fault coverage, the medical expenses would have been paid this way:

> Ethan's PIP on his own car would pay his $1,000 medical bill. If he was unable to work for a time after the accident, he could file a claim for lost wages against the remaining $9,000 provided by his $10,000 PIP.

*Frank's PIP on his own car would pay his $1,000 medical bill. Like Ethan, Frank could file a claim for lost wages against the remaining PIP coverage.*

*Gina's PIP on her own car would pay the first $10,000 of her $35,000 bill. To recover the remaining $25,000, she would have to file a claim against Mike's bodily injury liability coverage. Since his liability policy is inadequate to cover her expenses and probable lost income, Gina would have to sue for the balance.*

*Helen's PIP on her own car would pay the first $10,000 of her $100,000 bill. To recover the remaining $90,000, she would have to file a claim against Mike's bodily injury liability coverage. Since his liability policy is inadequate to cover her expenses and probable lost income, Helen, too, would have to sue for the balance.*

Because Gina and Helen used their full PIP coverage to pay medical bills, they would not be able to file a claim for any type of therapy, rehabilitation, or lost wages against their PIP.

Many insurance companies allow the consumer to buy additional PIP coverage for an added premium.

Oftentimes an agent will suggest PIP with a deductible in order to offer the client a lower premium. If PIP is purchased with a deductible, the insured person is responsible for the amount of the deductible before the PIP pays anything. Consider what would happen to Frank if he bought his policy with a $2,000 deductible on his PIP coverage:

*If Frank had a $2,000 deductible, he would have to pay his $1,000 medical bill with his own money. If he also required $999 of physical therapy, he would have to pay for that with his own money, too. His PIP would pay nothing* *until he has personally paid $2,000 out of pocket for accident related injury expenses.*

## Medical Coverage

In the states that do not require PIP, drivers are often required to buy medical coverage. This endorsement will pay for the medical bills incurred by the insured driver and any passengers in his or her car. To illustrate, we will assume that Mike lives in a state that does not require PIP. We will also assume that Mike bought a $50,000 medical coverage endorsement.

> *As a result of his collision with Ethan's car, Mike required medical treatment that cost $15,000. Mike's wife, who was in his passenger seat, required treatment that cost $11,000. Mike's medical coverage would pay both his and her medical bills up to the limits of the policy; that is, $50,000.*

If Mike had been driving a friend's car when he had this accident, the insurance purchased by the owner of that car would pay these bills. This is why agents will often warn the owner of a vehicle that when you loan your car, you also loan your insurance.

If Mike's car had been struck by an additional car, his own medical coverage would pay his doctor bills even though the other driver was the at fault driver. Then, Mike's insurance company would attempt to recover that money from the at fault driver's insurance company through a process called *subrogation*.

One additional point should be noted here. It is not uncommon for a person's health insurance to refuse to pay medical bills that are the result of an auto accident until the individual's PIP or Medical Coverage has paid its full amount. Also important to note, under no circumstances should the medical coverage provided by a person's auto insurance be considered a substitute for health insurance.

## Collision Coverage

When a car is damaged in an accident and either the driver is the at fault driver *or* the vehicle was damaged by a hit-and-run driver, collision coverage pays to repair it. Collision coverage nearly always has a deductible; the policy owner must pay a specified amount before the insurance policy pays for repairs. Deductibles are commonly $250, $500, $1,000, or more. The advantage of a higher deductible is the significant reduction in the premium. However, when a high deductible is selected, it is extremely important to have sufficient money in reserve, in a savings account for example, in order to pay the deductible when an accident occurs.

> *Let's assume that raising the deductible from $500 to $1,000 reduces the premium by $100 per year. Let's also assume that the policyholder has $500 in a savings account with which to pay the deductible. If the policyholder deposits that $100 premium reduction into that savings account for each of the next five years, the balance is increased from $500 to $1,000. Once this has been done, that $100 annual savings can now be used for something else.*

## Comprehensive Coverage

Collisions are not the only things that can damage cars. Fires, vandalism, and natural disasters, such as hail storms and tornadoes, can also damage cars, as can a collision with a wild animal like a deer. Comprehensive coverage pays to repair many different kinds of damage (including damage to glass); that's why it's called comprehensive.

If the car is stolen, comprehensive coverage pays the cost of replacing the car. The amount of payout is determined by the fair market value of the car that was stolen. For example, let's look at Marianne's options:

*Marianne's five-year-old Acme sedan was stolen while she was shopping at the mall. The replacement value is determined to be $5,000. This is the amount that she will be paid toward the cost of a replacement vehicle. If she can find an identical five-year-old Acme sedan, she can buy the car with the $5,000. On the other hand, if she decides to buy a brand new Acme sedan, or any other car, the $5,000 can serve as the down payment, reducing the amount that she has to pay or finance.*

Like collision coverage, comprehensive coverage typically has a deductible. The amount of the deductible can be the same as the deductible on the collision, a greater amount, or a lesser amount. Again, a higher deductible results in a lower premium.

One important point should be noted regarding the replacement of glass and deductibles. In some states, insurance companies are not permitted to charge a deductible to replace a windshield. Be sure to ask your insurance agent about the law in your state.

## Uninsured Motorist Coverage

While all states have laws that require drivers to purchase automobile insurance, there are people who violate the law by driving without insurance. Others who do purchase insurance get only the minimum required coverage and are actually underinsured for the damage they can cause in an accident. If you are involved in an accident with one of these drivers, you might find that their insurance is insufficient to repair or replace the damage done to you and your vehicle.

Uninsured Motorist Coverage, also referred to as UM, stands in place of the at fault driver's liability insurance when there is no insurance or too little insurance.

*In the accident between Ethan and Mike above, it is clear that Mike has insufficient liability coverage. If Ethan has purchased an uninsured motorist endorsement, his UM will now step up and help Gina and Helen with their medical bills, up to the limits of Ethan's UM coverage.*

It is important to note here that when Ethan's uninsured motorist coverage helps Gina and Helen with their medical bills, this does not end Mike's ultimate responsibility for them. After paying these costs, Ethan's insurance company will attempt to recover its money through the *subrogation* process and, if necessary, can sue Mike to recover whatever it can.

When purchasing uninsured motorist coverage, the consumer selects the amount of insurance he wants in the same way as for liability coverage. As a general rule, drivers cannot purchase more insurance in UM than they have purchased in liability coverage. In other words, policyholders cannot provide better protection for themselves than they are willing to provide for others.

*Roderick has informed his insurance agent that he wants to buy car insurance with liability coverage of 25/50/25 ($25,000 per person to a maximum of $50,000 per accident with $25,000 of property damage liability coverage). He also wants to buy uninsured motorist coverage. The maximum amount he will be able to buy is 25/50. If he chooses, Roderick can buy a lesser amount of protection, but he cannot exceed the amount of coverage he is providing for the general public.*

In some states, consumers are allowed to purchase stacked UM coverage. Here's how it works.

*Roderick has purchased UM coverage in the amount of 25/50, and he owns two cars. If he is in a state that allows the purchase of stacked coverage, he would be well advised to ask for it. Then, if he is involved in an accident with someone who has no insurance, or too little insurance, he can combine the UM coverage on each vehicle so that, in essence, he now has 50/100 uninsured motorist coverage.*

## Loss of Use/Rental Car Coverage

When your car is damaged in an accident and must be repaired, you still have to get from point A to point B. So how do you get around?

Loss of Use/Rental Car Coverage pays a specified amount of money on a per day basis to provide a rental car that can be used while the damaged vehicle is being repaired. Obviously, there is a limit to how much will be paid. The rented vehicle is usually comparable to the one that was damaged and is under repair. If the policyholder wants to upgrade to a luxury car, he or she will have to pay the difference in the rental rate.

## Towing and Labor Coverage

Sometimes cars break down, tires go flat, and gas tanks are empty. When these things happen, we need help—someone we can call right now. Towing and Labor Coverage provides that help. A rescue vehicle will bring the gas, change the tire, or tow the car to a nearby repair shop.

A cautionary note: when a policyholder uses this coverage, some companies consider it to literally be a claim filed against the policy. If a person files too many claims, the insurance company can raise the premiums or cancel the policy altogether. What's more, if a person has a history of filing many claims and tries to change companies, premiums will probably not be the lowest. A person electing to purchase this coverage as part of an auto insurance policy should first find out if using this coverage is considered to be filing a claim against the policy.

## Gap Insurance

In a perfect world, the amount we owe on a car would never be greater than what we could actually sell the car for. Alas, we do not live in a perfect world. Often, especially during the first part of the loan period, the amount owed far exceeds the value of the car that collateralizes the debt. If this is the situation when a car is determined to be a total loss ("totaled") by the insurance company, the owner will receive less money than is needed to pay off the loan. Gap insurance solves this problem by paying the difference so that the debt is paid in full.

> *Natalie owns a two-year-old vehicle. She borrowed $25,000 at the time of purchase and, after twenty-four monthly payments, she still owes $24,317. When her car was totally destroyed in a traffic accident last month, it had a trade-in value of $15,650. Before she can buy a new car, Natalie must pay off her existing car loan. Under normal circumstances, her insurance company would give her a check for $15,650 leaving her $8,667 short of being able to pay off the loan.*

However, because Natalie had the foresight to have a Gap Coverage endorsement added to her insurance policy, the insurance company will write a check for the full balance, $24,317, and she will be able to go car shopping with no residual debt hanging over her financial head.

## How Premiums Are Determined

Several factors are used to determine the premium for an auto insurance policy.

- **Policy limits**—the amount of coverage you get in each category. Key to remember is that liability coverage is extremely inexpensive—buy all you can get.

- **Deductibles**—what you pay before insurance kicks in. While low deductibles may feel comfortable, they almost always mean higher premiums. Conversely, higher deductibles generally mean lower premiums. As mentioned previously, drivers who have had few claims during their driving years may choose a higher deductible and put the savings in an account that will cover the deductible if there is an accident. In just a few years, that amount will accumulate, and the premiums savings can then be used for some other purpose.

- **Traffic citations**—the number and types issued. The real concern in this category is moving violations; not all violations are the same. For example, a ticket for driving 10 mph over the limit on the interstate is far less severe that a citation for driving 10 mph over the limit in a school zone. Violations have different point values based on the severity of the infraction and the dangers they create for both the driver and others. The most severe infractions include driving while intoxicated or under the influence of drugs, reckless driving, reckless homicide, and driving with a suspended license. The greater the number of moving violations and increasing severity of the infractions will cause premiums to escalate, or will make purchasing a policy virtually impossible.

- **Claims**—the number that have been filed and the cost of resolving them. This factor should give a policyholder pause for thought before filing a claim. Consider whether the payout will be high enough to warrant two possible consequences: (1) a possible hike in premium and (2) the insurance company's record of a claim being filed. For example,

  *A side window on Robert's car was broken, and the cost of replacing the glass was $275. Since he had a $250 deductible, filing this claim would not benefit him much. What's worse, however, is that the*

*insurance company will keep the claim filing on re-
cord, which could impact Robert's future premiums.*

- **Credit scores**—the higher the better. Because insurance companies have found that low credit scores are a predictor of
the number of claims a person is likely to file during the life
of a policy., many companies now use credit scores or credit
based insurance scores to determine the premium that a consumer will pay. It should be understood that the probability
of filing a claim is not the same as the probability of having
an accident.

  Nearly all states allow the use of these credit based insurance scores, and a great many companies use them as a key
factor in setting premiums. For some companies, in fact, it is
the only factor. This is a good example of why it is important
to periodically check your credit reports to ensure that they
are accurate, and to pay bills on time to avoid a low credit
score.

- **The vehicle symbol**—a numeric value that tells insurance companies more than you can imagine. A car's symbol tells how
well it holds up under a crash, how well it protects the passengers inside the car, the cost of repairs, and the probability
that the car will be stolen. If you are trying to decide which car
to purchase, it is a good idea to ask your insurance agent to tell
you the symbol of each car under consideration. You'll need the
car's vehicle identification number to obtain the symbol. When
comparing symbols, think of a game of golf—the lower the
score, the better the game. In this game, lower symbols mean
lower premiums.

- **Replacement parts**—the kinds of parts allowed to be used
to repair damage. Some insurance policies require the use of
only original manufacturer parts, also known as OEM parts, to

repair the damage from an auto accident. Others allow the use of parts made by other manufacturers to repair the damage. Known as after-market parts, these parts must meet or exceed the original manufacturer's specifications regarding fit and finish. As a general rule, after-market parts are less costly than OEM parts, allowing the insurance company to repair the car at a lower cost. That savings is passed on to policyholders in the form of lower premiums.

Here are steps that you can take to reduce the cost of car insurance:

- Ask your agent to help you compare the symbols of the cars you are considering.

- Select higher deductibles, but be sure to keep enough money in savings to pay that deductible if you have an accident.

- Build a good credit history with a good credit score.

- Shop around; compare different companies; ask friends and family members for recommendations of agents who can become trusted advisors and the companies that they represent.

- Check with the state insurance department to find out how many complaints a particular company or agent has had.

- Check with independent insurance agents who have access to many companies so they can help you find the best price.

## What to Do When You Have an Accident

Collect information

- The other driver's name

- The other driver's address

- The other driver's license number

- Names and contact information of any and all witnesses

- The name of the other driver's insurance company and policy number

- Call the police and get a police report

- Make note of any citations issued.

Take photographs of the scene and all damage to the vehicles. They provide a visual record of the accident and may prove helpful in determining who was at fault and any previous damage that was not caused by the accident

## What *Not* to Do When You Have an Accident

- Don't jump to the conclusion that what appears to be "minor" damage won't be expensive to repair.

- Don't assume that because you feel okay immediately after the accident that you have no injuries. Some injuries don't become apparent until one to three days after the accident. Have your doctor check you over.

- Don't say "I'm sorry." Doing so creates the immediate impression that you believe that you caused the accident. Let the police investigation assign responsibility for the accident.

- Don't file a claim for an amount that will be less than the deductible. You'll end up paying the entire bill anyway, but the insurance company will keep it on record as a filed claim.

# CONCLUSION

An auto insurance policy is comprised of many parts. Some of these parts are required by law while others are components that you can choose to add. Briefly, the various parts are

- **Liability Coverage**

    o When you are the "at fault driver," **Bodily Injury Liability** protects against the financial damages that are incurred when another person is hurt in an accident. Typically, this pays for medical bills and similar economic losses that the injured person incurs.

    o When you are the "at fault driver," **Property Damage Liability** pays to repair the other person's property.

- **Personal Injury Protection (PIP)** is required in some states and pays the insured person's medical bills, lost wages, and similar financial losses regardless of who was at fault in the accident. Some states refer to this as "no fault" coverage.

- In states that do not require PIP, **Medical Coverage** pays the medical bills for the "at fault driver" of the vehicle and his or her passengers.

- **Collision Coverage** pays to fix your car when you are the driver who caused the accident.

- **Comprehensive Coverage** pays to fix your car when it is damaged by fire, vandalism, or a collision with a wild animal. It also pays to repair or replace broken glass on the car.

- If you have the misfortune of being involved in an accident with someone who has no insurance or has too little insurance, **Uninsured Motorist Coverage** acts like the "at fault driver's" bodily injury liability protection to pay the same expenses as his or her insurance would have paid if he or she had been properly insured.

- While your car is being fixed after an accident, you still need transportation. **Loss of Use/Rental Car Coverage** will pay for a rental car (for a limited number of days) while your car is in the shop.

- **Towing and Labor Coverage** pays for roadside assistance. But be careful! When you use this coverage, some companies treat it just like any other claim you make against the policy.

- When you buy a new car, the value of that car goes down the minute you drive it off the showroom floor. If you have an accident in which the car is a total loss, you might owe more on the loan than the car is worth. **Gap Insurance** pays the difference between the car's value and the loan balance so you don't have to take money out of savings to make up the difference.

The price you pay for your insurance is also somewhat under your control. Several factors can lower the cost of auto insurance:

- Choosing lower policy limits

- Choosing higher deductibles that lower the amount you pay for comprehensive and collision coverage

- Employing safe driving habits so that you don't receive traffic tickets

- Avoiding frivolous or minimal claims

- Ensuring that your credit report is accurate, and paying bills on time to avoid a low credit score

- Choosing a vehicle with a symbol that the insurance company believes indicates lower risk

- Allowing after-market replacement parts

- Shopping wisely for a good insurance company and agent. Get referrals from friends who are happy with their agent and their insurance company.

- Checking with state regulators for complaints filed against an agent or company

- Asking an independent agent to help you compare many companies to find you the best price

A final reminder regarding premiums: while some people think they will save a lot of money by accepting very low policy limits on their liability coverage, liability coverage is cheap, cheap, cheap. The wise auto owner purchases the highest affordable liability coverage. The price difference between the "bargain basement" (minimum coverage) and the "penthouse" is seldom more than pennies a day.

Know what to do and what not to do if you have an accident.

Insurance

## CHAPTER 9

# Life and Disability Insurance

*Protecting Your Family Against the Risks of Your Dying Too Soon or Losing Your Ability to Earn a Living*

"The value of life is not in the length of days, but in the use we make of them; a man may live long yet very little."

— Michel de Montaigne

On the day that someone becomes a breadwinner for a family—be it for a spouse, children, or both—a huge responsibility descends onto his or her shoulders, one that is borne for the remainder of life and beyond. For this reason, the breadwinner must take the appropriate actions to protect loved ones against the risk of dying too soon or becoming disabled and unable to earn a living. How these risks are met and managed is a mark of maturity and responsibility.

# Life Insurance

Dr. Solomon Huebner, often called the father of life insurance education, taught the first course on life insurance at the University of Pennsylvania and founded the American College of Life Underwriters in the 1920s. The core of his texts on life insurance was the concept of Human Life Value, the value of a person to his or her family.

Lest anyone misinterpret this as an attempt to calculate the value of a human life, it is actually the calculation of the value of a person's contributions to the support of his or her family.

Imagine for a moment that you own a printing press that *legally* prints money for you—all you need do is turn it on each morning. Would you insure it against breakdown? Of course you would! How much would you insure it for? To decide that, you'd have to figure out how much money it could print every day and how many days you expect the machine to work.

That is precisely the concept of Human Life Value. The most valuable asset any of us owns is our ability to get out of bed and go to work in order to earn money. *We* are the press that prints money every day of our lives; the money that our families depend on for food, shelter, and clothing. The goal of life insurance is to replace the income that a person would have earned throughout his or her lifetime, should he or she pass away. How much money our family will need will be dependent on a number of circumstances.

Since everyone's needs are different, it should come as no surprise that there are different types of life insurance to meet the variety of needs.

## Needs

The amount of life insurance that a person needs is determined by the stage of life that individual is currently in. For example,

*Rodney just graduated from college. He is single and has no children. Some would say that because he has no dependents, he has no need for life insurance. However, consider these questions.*

- *If Rodney died tomorrow, who would pay for his funeral and burial?*

- *If Rodney owes money for anything, including student loans, mortgage, or car payment, where will be money come from to pay these debts?*

- *If Rodney feels strongly about his church or a specific charity and planned to make annual donations to fund their good work, who will step up to replace his commitments and continue the work that he felt was so vital?*

*These questions point out Rodney's need for life insurance. He will need*

- ***Final Expense Money**—while it is likely that Rodney's parents (assuming that they are still living) will come forward to bear this expense, should they really have to? What if they don't have the money available to cover it? Perhaps a lender will loan them the money. Losing a child is a painful enough occurrence; can you think of anything more heartbreaking than to be reminded of that loss every month when another payment comes due? Life insurance will provide the cash to pay these expenses, if a sufficient amount is purchased.*

- ***Cleanup Fund**—sadly, not only did Rodney still owe money on the car he bought before graduation, he also had taken out student loans. Worse still, some of those student loans were taken out by his parents using their own credit. Where will the money come from to repay these* *debts?* Life insurance will provide the funds to repay these debts, in full, if a sufficient amount is purchased.

- **Charitable Bequests**—*Rodney was very active in his church and supported the church's youth ministry. Even while he was in school, he contributed money to support this ministry every year. He fully intended to continue, in fact increase, his annual contributions now that he had graduated.* Life insurance can provide the money to fulfill his commitments and even establish a charitable bequest that will make Rodney's contribution every year even after he is gone if a sufficient amount is purchased.

In this case, Rodney's need for life insurance is relatively modest. Compare Rodney's situation with the couple below. Clearly, their situation is different from his, so their insurance needs are quite different; and yet, there are also some similarities.

*John and Linda are in their mid-thirties, are buying a house, and have two children ages 10 and 7. Here are their insurance needs.*

- **Final Expense Money**—*in the event that either John, Linda, or both should die, there will definitely be a need to pay the final expenses of a funeral and burial.* Life insurance will provide the cash to pay these expenses, if a sufficient amount is purchased.

- **Cleanup Fund**—*like most young couples, John and Linda have debts. While they are still making payments on their student loans, they also have taken on credit card debt. Moreover, should one of them die, the other will still be responsible for repaying the mortgage loan on the house. While it is not a certainty that the surviving partner will want to remain in the house without the other, what is certain is that the survivor will want to have the opportunity to make a choice rather than* *being forced into a decision that he or she has no desire to make.* Life insurance will provide the funds to repay these debts, in full, if a sufficient amount is purchased.

- **Income Replacement**—*as is the case for most young couples, they are a two-partner financial team. The family depends on both incomes to meet the costs of living. In order for the family to continue in the lifestyle to which they have become accustomed, the monthly earnings of either partner must be replaced if one them dies.* Life insurance can replace the income of the financial partner who is no longer alive to contribute to the success of the team, if a sufficient amount is purchased.

- **College Funds**—*as parents who both had to work their way through school with part-time jobs and summer employment supplemented by student loans, John and Linda have promised themselves that their children won't have to do the same thing. Their dream is for the children to be able to devote themselves to their studies and to graduate from college debt free.* Life insurance can keep that dream alive even if either of them, or both of them, should die before the dream becomes a reality, if a sufficient amount is purchased.

- **Charitable Bequests**—*John and Linda are both active in charitable works in their community contributing both time and money.* Life insurance can continue their financial contributions for many years to come when either or both die, if a sufficient amount is purchased.

Clearly, John and Linda have much different needs from Rodney. They have greater responsibilities and broader obligations than he does. But, for all of their differences, they all still would leave financial voids in need of filling.

A single parent also has much in common with John and Linda. Let's consider Helen.

*Helen is a single parent with three children, ages 9, 7, and 5. Because her late husband had not made suitable arrangements, she has been forced to work two jobs and manage her money very carefully in order to make certain that her children don't go without. Her needs are different from John and Linda's and yet they share similarities.*

- **Final Expense Money**—*as with John and Linda, there will definitely be a need to pay the final expenses of a funeral and burial.* Sufficient life insurance will provide the cash to pay these expenses.

- **Cleanup Fund**—*as with John and Linda, Helen has debts that must be repaid.* Sufficient life insurance will provide the funds to repay these debts, in full.

- **Income Replacement**—*Helen's need for income is markedly different. She has to consider who will raise her children if she dies. She* wants *someone who will put the children's needs first, who will raise them in accordance with her values, and who will love and protect them. She* needs *someone who has the financial resources to permit that person or couple to do all the things she* wants *them to do.* Fortunately, sufficient life insurance can provide a monthly income that will allow her to select a guardian who can satisfy her desires for her children without having to worry about how to also meet the financial requirements of doing so.

- **College Funds**—*just as John and Linda have promised themselves that their children won't have to work their way through school and be responsible for repaying student loans, Helen has the same dream for her children.*

Sufficient life insurance can keep that dream alive even if Helen is no longer here to make that dream a reality.

- **Charitable Bequests**—*Helen recognizes that she has been blessed to have help from others when she has needed it. She has vowed to provide the same assistance to others in their times of need.* Sufficient life insurance can provide funding to the organizations that Helen is helping now and/or may want to support in the future.

The needs of a mature couple whose children are no longer in the home are, in some ways, quite similar to those of a younger couple. However, they are different in that there is no longer a need to provide funds for raising children. Let's consider Ed and Sheila.

*Ed and Sheila are "empty-nesters." The children are grown and now raising families of their own. While each continues to work, they are looking forward to retirement and are making plans to ensure that they will be secure in their golden years. As they make these plans, let's examine their insurance needs.*

- **Final Expenses, Cleanup Fund, and Charitable Bequests**—*as with every other example we have examined, there will be need for money to pay final expenses, repay debts, and make charitable contributions after death.*

- **Income Replacement**—*planning for income replacement becomes a little more complicated at this stage of life. While Ed and Sheila still need to think in terms of replacing a lost paycheck in the event of a death while one partner is still working, there is now the issue of ensuring adequate retirement income when their working days are over. This latter concept is known as Pension Maximization.*

- **Pension Maximization**—*when a person retires, a decision must be made regarding the withdrawal of money from retirement plans. For the sake of simplicity, the term "retirement plan" will be used as a stand-in for all retirement plans, including company provided pension plans, 401k plans, 403b plans, and 457 plans.*

  *Nearly all retirement plans will offer the retiree a choice of how to receive money from the plan. For illustrative purposes, let us assume that Ed has $250,000 in his pension plan. His choices include[7]*

  o *Life Only Income—this option will provide a monthly income of $1,427 for as long as Ed lives. No more payments will be made by the pension plan following his death.*

  o *Life Income with Reduced Payment to Survivor—this option will pay Ed an income of $1,372 per month for long as he lives. If Ed dies before Sheila, she will continue to receive a pension check, but it will be reduced to $686 per month.*

  o *Joint and Last Survivor Income—this option will provide an income of $1,192 per month as long as either Ed or Sheila is alive.*

  *While Ed would certainly like to have the largest amount possible each month, he wants to continue to provide for Sheila after he's gone. Consequently, he must accept a*

---

[7] The numbers used in this example are for illustrative purposes only. The actual payout received by a retiree will be dependent on the amount of money in the plan, interest rates in effect at the time payments begin, the age of any co-beneficiary, and any other payment options that may be available within the plan. This illustration assumes that both parties were born on the same day.

*lesser income ($235 less) in order to provide Sheila with the same amount of money each month after his death. Further complicating the decision is the fact that, once Ed has made the selection, he cannot change it, even if Sheila dies before he does.*

*But what if there was a way for Ed to receive the larger income while he's alive and give Sheila the same income after his death?*

*To do this, Ed would have to purchase a life insurance policy that would give Sheila a lump sum of money that could be invested to generate a monthly income of $1,427. Ed could then accept the higher monthly income secure in the knowledge that Sheila's lifestyle would not suffer if he dies before her.*

## Types of Life Insurance

Just as there are different needs for life insurance, there are different types of life insurance to meet those needs.

**Term Insurance** provides a specific amount of protection for a specific amount of time. Generally speaking, it is used to meet "temporary" needs.

*In our example above, John and Linda have two children, ages 10 and 7. Their greatest need for insurance is to en-sure that the needs of the children are met until they are of age and can support themselves. This is considered a temporary need.*

Term insurance offers protection for a specified number of years. For example, an annual term policy provides coverage for one year; a five-year term policy provides coverage for five years; and so on for ten years, twenty years, etc. At the end of the term, the policy expires and no further obligation exists. The person who was insured is no longer required to pay premiums, and the insurance company provides no further protection. If the insurance contract includes the right to renew the policy, the policy can be renewed for an additional period of time equal to the initial term. Of course, the premium will be higher because the insured person is now older.

Term insurance can be level term or decreasing term. In a level term policy, the death benefit remains the same throughout the term of the contract. In a decreasing term policy, the death benefit decreases each year according to a schedule provided by the contract. The monthly premium for both level term and decreasing term remains the same throughout the duration of the term.

Some will ask why anyone would purchase a policy in which the amount of protection decreases while the premium remains the same. One reason could be that a decreasing death benefit is appropriate when the need that it is intended to cover is also decreasing; for example, a home mortgage loan in which the principle owed decreases as the loan is paid down.

**Permanent Life Insurance** offers a specified amount of protection that remains the same throughout the lifetime of the insured for a premium that also stays the same for the insured's lifetime. Just as there are different types of term insurance, there are also different types of permanent insurance.

- Traditional **Whole Life** provides a death benefit that remains the same throughout the lifetime of the insured, and premiums never change. The policy builds contractually guaranteed cash values that are calculated using an internal rate of return (interest rate) set by the insurance company. Cash value is the amount of money that would be paid to the policy owner if he or she returned it to the company stating that the policy is no longer wanted or needed. Cash value is usually less than the total premiums that have been paid to the company, especially in the early years of the policy. In fact, whole life policies typically do not contain any cash value for the first two to three years.

A Whole Life policy may pay dividends if the policy is "partici-pating;" that is, if it allows the policy owner to participate in a profit enjoyed by the insurance company that issued the policy. Dividends are never guaranteed.

- **Universal Life** differs from Whole Life in that while the cash value in the latter is contractually guaranteed and determined by the internal rate of return set by the insurance company, the cash value in the Universal Life policy will be determined by the earnings of the company's investments. In other words, they may go up or down, and cannot be predicted.

  Universal Life also differs from a Whole Life policy in that while the Whole Life policy pays only the death benefit, a Universal Life policy offers the insured a choice of providing the policy's beneficiary with the death benefit (Option A) or with the death benefit PLUS the cash value (Option B).

  The illustrations below show how the cash values and death benefits are impacted by the selection of Option A versus Option B.

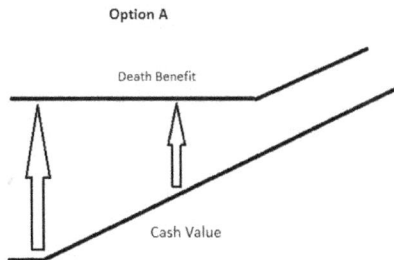

Option A

Death Benefit

Cash Value

As Cash Value increases, the amount of insurance that must be paid for decreases. Cash Value cannot exceed the death benefit. So the death benefit must increase in order to maintain the "corridor of risk."

FIGURE 9.1

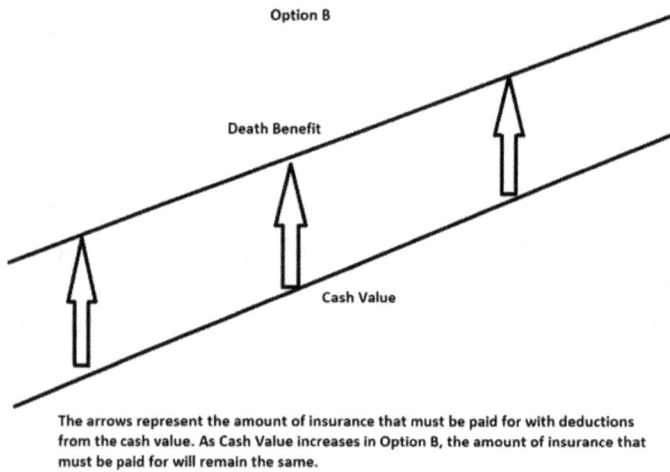

The arrows represent the amount of insurance that must be paid for with deductions from the cash value. As Cash Value increases in Option B, the amount of insurance that must be paid for will remain the same.

FIGURE 9.2

As Cash Values increase, they cannot exceed the death benefit because doing so would violate the tax laws that mandate the tax-sheltered treatment that cash values receive. To maintain the corridor of risk, Option A must allow the death benefit to increase if the Cash Value too closely approximates the death benefit.

Each month the policy owner pays the monthly premium. This money goes into the cash value "bucket." Each month the insurance company credits interest into the same bucket based on the amount of money in the bucket and the current interest rate being paid by the company.

Each month the insurance company takes money from the bucket to pay the cost of insurance; that is, how much it costs to insure the life of that individual for that month. As the insured gets older, the cost of insurance goes up each year.

The insurance company also takes money from the bucket to pay the cost of any riders that have been added to the policy. Examples of riders include an accidental death benefit which would pay an extra amount if death is the result of an accident, or a waiver of premium benefit which would pay the monthly premiums if the insured became sick or disabled for a specified period of time and was unable to work.

Finally, the insurance company collects money from the bucket to pay the cost of maintaining the policy.

This illustration below shows how a Universal Life policy works.

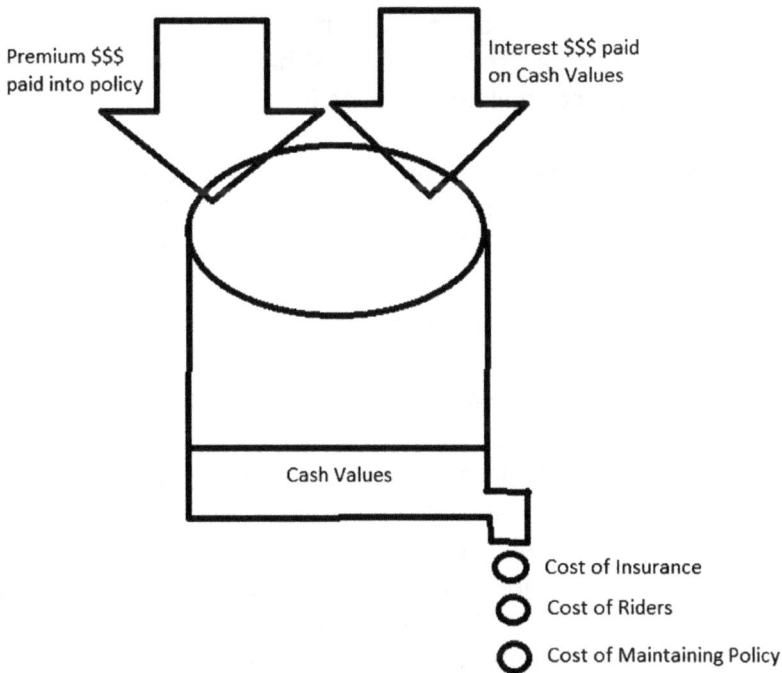

Premium $$$ paid into policy

Interest $$$ paid on Cash Values

Cash Values

◯ Cost of Insurance
◯ Cost of Riders
◯ Cost of Maintaining Policy

FIGURE 9. 3

The advantage offered by Universal Life is that when market interest rates are greater than the internal rate of return that was used to calculate the guaranteed cash values in a Whole Life Policy, the Universal Life policy will allow the policy owner to earn the market interest rate and build greater Cash Values. It also allows flexibility in premium payments. The policy owner has the option to pay more than the planned monthly premium thereby accelerating the Cash Value buildup. The policy owner also has the option of paying less than the planned monthly premium. Doing so could cause the Cash Value to build more slowly or to decrease.

The disadvantage of a Universal Life policy, however, is that if the market interest rates decrease to the point where money going into the bucket is less than the money coming out of the bucket, ultimately the Cash Value will be exhausted. Should that happen, the policy will collapse and the insurance will no longer be in force.

**Variable Universal Life** is based on the same premise as Universal Life. Monthly premium payments go into the bucket and monthly deductions are taken from the bucket to pay the cost of insurance, cost of riders, and cost of maintaining the policy. The policy owner chooses to be insured under Option A or Option B.

The primary difference between Universal Life and Variable Universal Life is how the return on the Cash Value is determined. Where the insurance company sets the interest rate to be credited to the Cash Value in a Universal Life policy based on returns on the investments that the company selects, the owner of a Variable Life policy actually decides how those cash values are to be invested and assumes responsibility for the investment returns. To do this, the policy owner selects investments, called sub-accounts, from a list assembled by the insurance company. These sub-accounts can invest in the stocks of large, mid-size, and small companies, or in bonds issued by large corporations and government entities. Sub-accounts follow investment policies that are designed to govern the amount of risk that the money manager can take and the types of investments that can be made.

There are some who will argue that life insurance itself is just a gamble—the insured is betting that he or she is going to die soon and the insurance company is betting that the insured is going to live for a long time. In reality, insurance companies have a relatively good idea how many people of any age are going to die in a year. They base this idea on what is called a mortality table. Currently insurance companies use the Commissioners Standard Ordinary 2001 Mortality Table.

This table tells us, for example, that of every 1,000 men who turned 45 on their last birthday, 2.77 will die within the next twelve months. Although it cannot predict *who* will die, it does predict *how many* will die based on statistical information gathered from a large number of people.

Insurance premiums are based on this probability along with other factors. These other factors include the person's

- Height and weight

- Medical history

- Current health

## How Much Insurance You Need

The first decision that must be made is how much of your monthly income must be replaced. Will the surviving family need to replace your entire paycheck or just a portion of it? Multiply the monthly income needed by twelve to determine the annual need.

In general, there are two ways to earn money. You can get out of bed in the morning and go to work, or you can have money that goes to work for you. Therefore, if a person dies and can no longer earn money, invested money works to continue generating income. The next question is how much that money can earn. What rate of return can we anticipate on our investments? How much interest will the investments earn? Since we're talking about "widows and orphans" money here, we should not be taking a lot of risks with the investments. When the percentage of return on investment is known, that number, expressed as a decimal, is divided into the annual income needed. This will calculate the amount of money required to create the annual income needed. (See the equation below for George and Marianne Kirby.)

To this figure, add the money needed to pay for final expenses, repay debts, establish college funds for dependent children, and cover any charitable bequests that are to be made at death. The final number is the amount of insurance that is needed. Once again, an example can illustrate the final calculations.

> *George and Marianne Kirby are both non-smokers with two children, ages 1 and 3.*
>
> *George is 30 years old and works for the Drill 'Em Deep Well Company as the office manager. His annual income is $32,000. At 6' 1" and 195 pounds, George is in excellent health and his last physical, two months ago, confirmed that he is in great health.*
>
> *Marianne is 28 years old and works as a bookkeeper at the Ace Accounting Agency. She stands 5' 7" tall and weighs 140 pounds. Her last checkup revealed that she, too, is in great health.*
>
> *George and Marianne recently met with their attorney, Dewey Cheatham, who advised that they not only update their wills to reflect that they now have two children, but that they also purchase life insurance. He recommended that they talk with his insurance agent, Raymond Mazy at the Shifting Sands of Daytona Life Insurance Company.*
>
> *After talking with Mr. Mazy, they came to these decisions:*

- *In the event that George dies, Marianne will need to replace his entire paycheck. Since she is very conservative with her money, she believes that she could earn 5 percent on her investments. Therefore, to replace George's $32,000 income, she makes this calculation:*

$$\$32,000/.05 = \$640,000$$

*Annual Income Needed / Anticipated Earnings on Investment expressed as Decimal = Insurance Needed*

*To this amount, she must add money for*

  o *Final expenses ($10,000)*

  o *College expenses ($30,000) for each child based on current in state tuition at State University*

*When all of the figures are added together, they show that George must purchase a life insurance policy in the amount of $710,000.*

- *Should Marianne die, George realizes that he, too, must replace her entire paycheck in order to maintain the home that she has created for him and the children. Less conservative with his investments than Marianne, George believes he can earn a 7.5 percent return on his investments. To replace her income, he makes this calculation:*

$$\$27,000/.075 = \$360,000$$

*Like Marianne, he wants to allow $10,000 for final expenses and a college fund of $30,000 for each of the children. In total, Marianne must purchase a life insurance policy in the amount of $430,000.*

Mr. Mazy reviewed their needs and offered these suggestions.[8]

- **20 Year Renewable Term—**

  o This will be the least expensive coverage for George and Marianne to purchase.

    ➢ *For George, the monthly premium for $710,000 of coverage will be $58.75. At the end of year 20, he will have paid a total premium of $14,100. Because this is a pure term policy that does not anticipate paying a dividend, his net cost will be the entire $14,100.*

    ➢ *For Marianne, the monthly premium for $430,000 coverage will be $31.29. At the end of year 20, she will have paid a total premium of $7,509.60. Because this is a pure term policy that does not anticipate paying a dividend, her net cost will be $7,509.60.*

    ➢ *Total premiums to insure both George's*

---

[8] The policies and premiums illustrated reflect products and rates available at the time of this writing. The company whose products are cited is nationally known, rated AA+ (Superior) by A.M. Best (the second highest rating on a sixteen-part scale). Premiums assume that both individuals are non-smokers and qualify for standard rates.

and Marianne's life under this option are $90.04 per month.

- **A combination of $100,000 whole life and $610,000 20-year term—**

  o This policy will allow George and Marianne to enjoy the protection of the full amount of insurance needed and still build some Cash Value.

    ➢ George will pay a monthly premium of $92.56 for the Whole Life portion and $49.91 for the 20 Year Term portion; total premium cost, 142.47 per month. At the end of 20 years, he will have paid a total of $34,192.80. His guaranteed Cash Value will be $19,248. In addition to this, the non-guaranteed dividend is projected to be $8,786. Should he decide to surrender the policy (that is, stop paying premiums and give up the coverage) at this point, the insurance company would send him a check for $29,964 (cash value + dividends). When we subtract the amount of the cash value + dividend from the total premiums paid ($34,192.80 - $29,064), we find that the net cost for this policy was only $5,128.80 spread over the entire 20 years that the policy was in force.

    ➢ Marianne would pay $73.78 per month for $100,000 in Whole Life coverage and an additional $25.77 per month for the remainder in 20 Year Term portion;

*total premium cost, $99.55. At the end 20 years, she will have paid a total of $23,892. Her guaranteed Cash Value will be $19,429. In addition to this, the non-guaranteed dividend is projected to be $9,476. Should she decide to surrender the policy at this point, the insurance company would send her a check for $28,905 (cash value + dividends). When we subtract the cash value + dividend from the total premiums paid ($23,892 - 28,905) we find that Marianne actually has not a net cost, but rather a net gain of $5,013.*

- **Traditional Whole Life—**

  o This option will be the most costly in terms of the monthly premium, but it will also maximize the accumulation of cash value.

    ➢ *George will pay a monthly premium of $505.79 for a $710,000 policy; and at age 65, he will have paid a total premium of $212,431.80. But, by the time George reaches age 65, the policy will have a guaranteed Cash Value of $287,692. Assuming the current dividend scale, there will be an additional $78,920 in non-guaranteed dividends. Should he choose to cash in (surrender) the policy in at age 65, the combined Cash Value and dividends would be $388,437, or $176,023.20 more than he paid into the policy! One other fact should be taken into account. If, at* *any time between the ages of 30 and 65, George dies, his family will receive the $710,000 death benefit regardless of how many or how few premium payments are made after the initial payment!*

➤ *For Marianne, the monthly premium to buy all of her insurance coverage in a Whole Life policy will be $303.57. When she is age 65, the insurance policy will have a guaranteed Cash Value of $169,545. Once again, if we assume the current dividend scale, there would be an additional $124,292 in non-guaranteed dividends, yielding a total surrender value of $293,837. After subtracting the $127,499.40 that was paid as the total premium over 35 years, Marianne would have a net gain of $166,337.60! This is in addition to the fact that, as with George, had Marianne died between the ages of 28 and 65, the company would have paid her beneficiary (George) $430,000!*

Clearly, George and Marianne will need to determine which plan best fits their household budget before deciding which policy to buy. For them, and anyone else considering the purchase of an insurance policy, the most important point is to buy the amount of insurance that is *needed* at the price that best fits into their budget.

## Underwriting—Whether the Policy Can Be Issued

Underwriters evaluate the risks presented by every individual who applies for life insurance. They consider a great many factors to determine if the policy can be issued, and, if so, at what cost. Here is a short list showing a few of the questions they will be asking.

- What is your gender? Women tend to live longer than men, so their premiums tend to be lower than men's (all other things being equal).

- How is your general health? Any chronic health issues such as high blood pressure, high cholesterol, asthma, or diabetes might increase the risk of an early death.

- How tall are you and how much do you weigh? While you may not think you are overweight, the underwriter may believe that you are "under tall" for the weight you are carrying.

- Do you use any kinds of tobacco products? The risks associated with the use of tobacco are well documented and cause insurance companies to charge tobacco users (whatever the form of tobacco) much higher premiums than are charged for non-users of tobacco.

- Do you participate in any vocations or avocations that pose additional risk? Sky diving, skin or scuba diving below 40 feet, hang gliding, and similar activities pose risks that are greater than those encountered by people who do not pursue hazardous activities.

All of these factors and others will be reviewed before a decision is made to issue the policy, and, if it is issued, whether it will be issued at "standard" rates or if additional premiums will be charged due to the risk of premature death.

## Taxation of Life Insurance Benefits

Life insurance proceeds are not subject to federal *income* taxes when the policy is owned by the insured and the money is paid to a named beneficiary. However, the money received from a life insurance policy may be subject to federal and state *estate,* or *death,* taxes. Because tax law is always subject to change, it is advisable to discuss your specific situation with a tax professional to ensure that you do not receive an unpleasant surprise from the IRS or state tax collector.

As was mentioned at the beginning of this chapter, the most valuable asset anyone owns is the ability to get out of bed every morning and go to work and earn a living. This is the reason why life insurance is purchased—to protect families against the risk of premature death. But what happens when someone is so sick or injured that going to work is impossible? How can we protect a family against the possibility that this might happen?

## Disability Insurance

Disability Insurance, often referred to as Disability Income Insurance, is designed to replace a portion of a person's income when a prolonged illness or injury prevents him or her from going to work. No one expects to die any time soon, and even fewer people believe that they will suffer a prolonged illness or injury. The thought process is simple: "That won't happen to *me.* That kind of thing happens only to *other* people!" Reality, however, is an entirely different matter.

While *life insurance* underwriters look at the 2001 Commissioner's Standard Ordinary Mortality Tables to determine how many people in every 1,000 are likely to die, *disability insurance* underwriters use the 1985 Commissioner's Individual Disability Table A to determine the likelihood of a disability lasting 90 days or longer. When these tables are compared to each other, the statistics are startling. Look at these examples:

- A 25-year-old male who "knows" that he's indestructible is 32 percent more likely to have a disability lasting more than 90 days than he is likely to die.

- A 25-year-old female who also "knows" that she is indestructible is 147 percent more likely to have a disability lasting for more than 90 days than she is likely to die!

- The 35-year-old male, having matured enough to know that he's not indestructible, still "knows" that nothing bad is going to happen to him; he's young and healthy. The reality, though, is that, like the 25 year old, he is 32 percent more likely to face a disability of 90 days or longer than he is to die.

- The 35-year-old female is 135 percent more likely to suffer a disability of 90 days or longer than she is to die.[9]

In fact, the Commissioner's Individual Disability Table A tells us that the 25-year-old male faces an 80 percent probability of suffering a disability of at least 90 days at some time before he reaches age 65 while the 35-year-old male has a 67 percent likelihood of suffering a disability of 90 days or longer at some time before age 65.

When disability strikes, the wage earner's income usually stops, but the bills continue to come in. Depending on how the insurance policy is written, it will usually replace somewhere between 50 percent and 70 percent of the worker's income. An insurance company wouldn't want to write a policy that replaces 100 percent of the lost income for one simple reason: if the policy replaces my entire income, what incentive do I have to "get well"?

Because disability is such a very real possibility, common sense dictates that we must protect ourselves against this financially devastating event. But where should a person look for this solution?

---

[9] The statistics cited are probabilities only. Actual results are dependent on each individual's age, gender, occupation, health, and other factors.

Some people expect Social Security to provide the solution. However, the reality is that in 2010, less than 35 percent of all Social Security Disability applications were approved.[10]

Fortunately, many employers offer their employees the opportunity to purchase short-term and/or long-term disability coverage. While definitions vary from one policy to another, short-term is usually defined as a period of up to 6 months. Long-term disability is usually one lasting for more than 6 months. Purchasing this coverage through an employer sponsored plan is often a very cost effective way to obtain the insurance because the employer frequently receives lower group rates. In addition, in some cases, employers may pay a portion of the premium for their employees as a benefit designed to keep good workers with the company. If an employer does not offer this vital protection, it is advisable that each person buy an individual policy.

When considering the purchase of disability insurance policy, there are some key components to look for.

- **What is the definition of "disability"?** Different policies have different definitions and the way in which this word is defined can have a huge impact on both the protection the policy provides and the premium that the consumer is charged.

  o Defining the disability in the most restrictive manner ("own occupation"), **"the inability to do *your specific job,"** means that the policy will pay benefits even if the person could easily do another job. For example, a construction worker suffers a back injury and can no longer lift heavy objects. This person goes back to school and becomes an accountant. He or she would still be able to collect disability benefits because he or she can no longer work on construction projects. Since this definition is

---

[10] U.S. Social Security Administration Office of Retirement and Disability Policy Annual Statistical Report on the Social Security Disability Insurance Program 2011.

the one most likely to require that benefits be paid, it is also the most expensive coverage to purchase.

o   A less restrictive definition is **"the inability to perform any job for which the insured is qualified by experience and/or training."** In the example above, the construction worker would receive income benefits while attending school. Upon gaining employment as an accountant, the benefits would cease to be paid. Since a policy using this definition is probably going to make fewer payments or have fewer claims, it will be less expensive to buy than the policy using the more restrictive definition.

o   The least restrictive and least expensive disability policy ("any occupation") to purchase uses the definition **"the inability to perform any work."** The use of this definition poses a serious risk for the insured person in that it makes it very difficult to successfully claim benefits. Using our construction worker above, let's assume that the injury is so severe that the person is confined to bed for the remainder of life. The insurance company would still have the ability to deny a claim on the grounds that the worker is capable of making telephone calls and could work from home as a telephone solicitor.

- Is the policy **cancellable**? Can the insurance company cancel the policy for any reason? Or can only the policy owner cancel the coverage?

- Is the policy **guaranteed renewable**? Or, if the policy is in effect for only a specific number of years (much like a term life insurance policy), is the insurance company required to renew the policy if the policy owner wishes to do so?

- What is the **elimination period**? This is the waiting period before the payment of benefits begins. The longer the interval between the beginning of the injury or illness and the start of benefit payments, the lower the premium will be.

To illustrate, let's revisit George Kirby, our 30-year-old office manager at Drill 'Em Deep Well Company where his annual income is $32,000. As office manager, he works exclusively in the office and does no field work at all. Let's look at the policy options presented to George. In both cases, disability is defined as the inability to perform the substantial and material duties of the regular occupation; or, the inability to perform the substantial and material duties of another occupation for which the insured is qualified by experience, education, and training.

- Non-Cancellable and Renewable—in this policy, the insurance company guarantees that the policy will be renewed every year, that the premium will not change, and that the company cannot add any restrictions or riders after the policy is issued.

  o The policy will pay benefits up to age 65 if George becomes totally and permanently disabled.

  o The basic benefit is $2,000 per month.

  o There is a "social insurance benefit" of $810 per month. Should George be paid social security disability benefits (or benefits under any other social insurance program), this basic benefit will be reduced dollar for dollar by any benefits received from social security. Thus, he will receive $1,090 from the insurance company + the social insurance benefits of $810 for a total monthly income of $2,000.

  o Assuming that George does not receive benefits under any social insurance program, his monthly income from this policy will be $2,000 (75 percent of his normal income).

  o The policy has a 90-day elimination period.

o The monthly premium for this policy will be $50.01 per month.

If George changes the elimination period from 90 days to 180 days, the monthly premium will be reduced to $47.16 per month.

- Guaranteed Renewable—in this policy, the insurance company guarantees that the policy will be renewed every year. However, the insurance company has the right to change the premium with 30 days prior notice.

    o The policy will pay benefits up to age 65 if George becomes totally and permanently disabled.

    o The basic benefit is $2,000 per month.

    o There is a "social insurance" benefit of $810 per month. Should George be paid social security disability benefits (or benefits under any other social insurance program), he will receive $1,090 from the insurance company plus $810 from social security.

    o Assuming that George does not receive benefits under any social insurance program, his monthly income from this policy will be $2,000 (75 percent of his normal income).

    o The policy has a 90-day elimination period.

    o The monthly premium for this policy will be $43.16 per month.

    If George changes the elimination period from 90 days to 180 days, the monthly premium will be reduced to $40.73 per month.

As you can see from this example, the elimination period makes a difference in the premium as does whether the policy is non-cancellable or simply guaranteed renewable.[11]

People always want to know if benefits received under a disability income insurance policy are subject to income taxation. The answer is a definite "maybe."

- If the premiums for disability insurance coverage are *either* paid by the employer, *or* paid with untaxed money under a Section 125 "cafeteria plan" where the employer is giving the employee *untaxed* "benefits dollars" with which to pay for benefits selected by the worker from a menu of available benefits, the benefits from the disability insurance policy will be taxed as ordinary income.

- If the premiums for disability coverage are being paid for by the employee with *after-tax* dollars (even if the payments are made through payroll deductions), the benefits from the insurance policy will be not be taxable for federal income tax purposes.

In our example above, if disability income insurance is offered by the Drill 'Em Deep Well Company Section 125 "cafeteria plan," George will likely be presented with two choices.

*Option 1—George can elect to receive benefits equal to 70 percent of his income and pay the premiums using his "benefits dollars," or*

---

[11] The policies and premiums illustrated reflect products and rates available at the time of this writing. The company whose products are cited is nationally known, rated AA+ (Superior) by A.M. Best (the second highest rating on a sixteen part scale). Premiums assume that the individual is a non-smoker and qualifies for standard rates.

*Option 2—George can elect to receive benefits equal to 50 percent of his income and pay the premiums using after-tax money.*

While most people will instinctively say that George should select Option 1, he needs to do a little math before making his choice. Since Option 1 will result in benefits being taxed as ordinary income, George needs to determine his marginal tax rate and deduct the income tax he will have to pay from the benefits he will receive. If the result of this calculation is an after-tax benefit that is greater than 50 percent of his income, then Option 1 is the best choice. But if the after-tax benefit amount is less than 50 percent of George's income, he should choose Option 2 because it will give him more spendable money with which to pay his bills.

## Can I Get the Policy Issued and What Will It Cost?

While the primary concern for a life insurance underwriter is mortality (how likely the applicant is to die), the disability income insurance underwriter must look at morbidity (how likely the applicant is to suffer an illness or injury that prevents him or her from working for an extended period of time). Many factors go into this determination.

- How old is the applicant? As we age, our bodies become more prone to injury and illness.

- What is the applicant's gender? While women tend to live longer than men resulting in lower life insurance premiums, they are more likely to suffer an extended disability which results in higher premiums.

- What is the applicant's health history? Health problems don't always lead to death. All too often, they make it difficult if not impossible for the insured person to work and earn a living.

- What is the applicant's work classification? Different types of jobs present different risks of illness or injury. While this thought process is a bit of an oversimplification, perhaps the easiest way to measure the risk of disability is to ask this question. "Does the job require more physical effort or more mental effort?" As a general rule, greater physical effort will require higher premiums and the insurance will be more difficult to obtain.

## CONCLUSION

No one enjoys contemplating his or her own mortality. However, the prudent individual makes plans for this inevitability.

The purpose of life insurance is to protect people against the premature death of a breadwinner. While no one can truly place a value on a human being's life, the concept of the human life value attempts to determine the lifetime earning power of that breadwinner. This number is used to calculate the amount of life insurance needed to replace that individual's income. The life insurance provides the funds to replace lost income, plus

- Final expense money for funeral and burial bills

- Cleanup funds for outstanding debts

- Replace the bread winner's income

- College funds for children

- Charitable bequests that the person supported in life

- Pension maximization in retirement

Different types of life insurance are designed to meet different types of needs.

- Term insurance provides temporary coverage to meet temporary needs. It also provides the greatest amount of insurance protection for the lowest possible cost. However, the cost of the insurance can increase as the insured person gets older. Term insurance generally provides protection for a specific number of years; that is, 1 year, 5 years, 10 years, etc.

- Permanent insurance provides permanent coverage to meet permanent needs. Because it builds cash values, the cost of permanent insurance is higher than the cost for the same amount of term insurance. However, the premium is designed to remain the same throughout the person's lifetime. Permanent insurance is available as Whole Life, Universal Life, and Variable Universal Life. Each has its own advantages and disadvantages.

While your premium dollars pay for life insurance, your good health is what enables you to buy it. Underwriters review your health history to determine if the company is willing to provide the insurance protection requested.

Life insurance benefits are free from federal income taxes when paid to a named beneficiary. However, they may be subject to federal estate taxes.

Where life insurance protects your loved ones against the loss of your income due to death, disability insurance protects you and your loved ones against the loss of your income due to illness or injury. How disability is defined will determine your ability to receive benefits under the policy and the cost of the policy.

- An "own occupation" definition means that you are disabled if you cannot perform the normal duties of your specific job.

- A definition based on education and experience means that you are disabled if you cannot perform the normal duties of any job for which you are qualified based on your education, training, and experience.

- An "any occupation" definition means that you are disabled only if you cannot perform the normal duties of *any* kind of job.

Another factor that decides how much the policy costs is whether the policy can be canceled or renewed.

- Non-cancellable and renewable means only you can cancel the policy and the premium will remain the same as long as you own the policy.

- Guaranteed renewable means the insurance company must renew the policy for as long as you want to keep it, but the premiums could be increased with the passage of time.

Benefits paid under a disability income insurance policy will be taxable if the premiums are paid with untaxed dollars. However, if the insured person is paying the premiums with *after-tax* money, the benefits will not be subject to federal income taxes.

Some people will say, "I don't plan on getting hurt and being unable to work." Others will say, "When I'm dead, I won't need life insurance."

To the first group I offer the observation that no one plans on becoming disabled. That item never appears on someone's "To Do List"; and yet, it happens to people every day.

To the latter group, I offer the observation of a wise man I once knew. "Life insurance is meant for the living, not for the dead. It allows the survivors to continue in the lifestyle that the deceased made them accustomed to. It is the most sincere love letter a person can write to his or her family. It reads,

*"While I am no longer here with you, I still love you enough to provide for you and take care of you.*

*Love,*
*Me"*

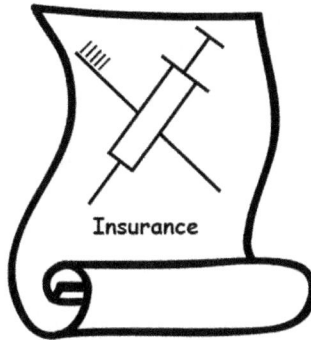

Insurance

CHAPTER 10

# Medical and Dental Insurance

*Can I Afford to Get Sick?*

"The doctor of the future will give no medicine but will interest his patients in the care of the human frame, in diet and in the cause and prevention of disease."

— Thomas Edison

Medical or Health Insurance is designed to protect families from the economic consequences of illness. As the cost of healthcare has risen, so too has the price for health insurance. It is imperative to understand the different types of policies and how they perform in the way they pay medical expenses.

## Types of Health Insurance

**Point of Service Policies (POS)**—in a point of service policy, the policy owner is free to select the doctor of his or her choice. There is no need to determine if the doctor is part of a network, no need to get permission from a "gatekeeper" to see a specialist. The policy owner sees the physician of choice, pays for the services delivered, and then files a claim with the insurance company for reimbursement.

Upon receipt of the claim, the insurance company reviews the services delivered and reimburses the policy owner an amount that is based on what the insurance company refers to as "reasonable and customary fees." Consider this example:

*Rocco Bilbao is a 47 year old who works as a construction supervisor for Strong Builders. For two days he has been running a fever with a sore throat and, because his son recently had strep throat, Rocco decides to see his doctor and make sure that he doesn't have strep throat, too. The doctor examines Rocco and determines that he does not have strep; it is simply a mild case of the flu. As Rocco leaves the doctor's office, he is presented with a bill for $100 and asked to pay it at that time, which he does.*

*Rocco now files a claim with his insurance company requesting reimbursement. Rocco's policy pays 80 percent of the reasonable and customary rate leaving him with a 20 percent co-payment, or co-pay. This means that he is responsible for $20, if the company considers $100 to be reasonable and customary.*

*However, if Rocco's insurance company has set the reasonable and customary rate at $80, they will reimburse him only $64 ($80 x 80 percent) so that he will also be responsible for the $16 difference. Consequently, this trip to the doctor will cost Rocco a total of $36.*

**Preferred Provider Organization (PPO)**—in a preferred provider network, the insurance company has already negotiated the price it will pay for medical services with physicians. When the doctor agrees to accept a negotiated fee, he or she becomes a preferred provider. This is also known as being "in network." Rocco can choose a primary care physician from a list of doctors who are in the network. If he wants to see a specialist, some policies will require that he get a referral from his primary care physician; others will not.

Let's re-examine Rocco's visit to the doctor if his insurance is a PPO plan.

> At the conclusion of Rocco's examination, he is presented with a bill for his co-pay. Since the policy calls for a $20 co-pay, Rocco pays the co-payment and the doctor's office bills the insurance company for the pre-negotiated fee.

If Rocco goes to a doctor who is not "in network," this policy will function similarly to a Point of Service Policy and he will end up being responsible for a higher co-payment amount.

In compliance with the Healthcare Reform laws passed in 2010, PPO plans now provide preventive care with no co-pay or deductible. The plan document will explain which services are deemed to be preventive and which are not.

**Health Maintenance Organization**—in a health maintenance organization, the doctor is typically an employee of the organization and is located in its facility. To some degree, this limits the patient's choices in that he or she can see only physicians and specialists who are employed by the HMO. In some HMOs, the patient will have a specific primary care physician; in others, the patient will see whichever doctor is on duty and available at the time of the visit. To schedule an appointment with a specialist, Rocco must obtain permission, a referral, from his primary care physician to one of the HMO's specialists. Once again, we can look at Rocco's visit to the doctor.

> Rocco's primary care physician has examined him and determined that there is no need for him to see a specialist. Rocco will pay a modest co-pay as he leaves the office. Because the doctor is an employee of the HMO, the transaction is finished and no further billing is necessary.

One of the largest differences between these plans, aside from how they pay the fees for services delivered, is how they treat preventative medical treatments. POS programs generally encourage treatment of patients after problems have arisen. HMOs, on the other hand, usually provide annual physicals and other preventive care in an effort to ward off illness before it happens. One caveat to selecting an HMO is that the primary care physician is sometimes incentivized not to refer patients to specialists.

In many instances, employer provided health insurance is often the most cost effective manner in which to obtain coverage. It benefits both the employer and the employee.

- The employer is probably obtaining coverage at group rates. This is especially valuable to individuals who have health issues that might otherwise cause an insurer to charge higher premiums or deny coverage altogether.

- In order to provide a benefit that will help the employer retain high quality employees and reduce turnover, many employers provide health insurance to employees at a lower rate by paying a portion of the premium for the employee.

## Health Insurance for Children

The Children's Health Insurance Program (CHIP) has been in existence since 1997. Each state administers its own CHIP that provides low cost or no cost healthcare to children in low and moderate (depending on current definitions as they relate to the federal poverty guidelines) income families. When a parent applies for medical coverage from a state agency on behalf of a child, the child is screened for both CHIP and Medicaid and placed in the appropriate program. Medicaid and CHIP typically provide

- Doctor visits

- Emergency care

- Hospital care

- Vaccinations

- Prescription drugs

- Vision care

- Dental care

- Hearing care

For information about the CHIP in your state, visit http://insurekidsnow.gov/.

## Dental Insurance

Just like medical insurance, dental insurance offers choices in the types of policies offered.

**Point of Service**—as with its medical insurance counterpart, the patient selects the dentist and pays for the services rendered. The patient then submits a claim for reimbursement to the insurance company, which in turn pays the contractual percentage of all reasonable and customary rates. If this is less than the fee charged by the dentist, the patient must pay an amount higher than the co-pay.

**Preferred Provider Organization**—as with its medical insurance counterpart, this dental insurance offers a network of dentists who have agreed to accept pre-negotiated fees, and the patient pays a small co-payment at the time of service. If a specialist such as an oral surgeon is required, it may or may not be necessary to obtain a referral from the primary care dentist. If an out-of-network dentist is used, the patient will be required to pay a higher co-payment due to the difference between the pre-negotiated fee and the fee charged by the out-of-network provider.

**Dental Health Maintenance Organization (DHMO)**—similar to the HMO, the dental health maintenance organization has dentists in their facility who are employees of the DHMO. The patient pays a small co-pay for each visit.

## Prescription Medications

Many health insurance plans provide some form of prescription medication coverage. As a general rule, these plans divide prescription drugs into three categories. The categorization will usually be along these lines.

- *Brand New* **Name Brand Drugs**—these are usually the newest, latest, and greatest drugs for some condition. Because they are under patent protection, the only manufacturer is the pharmaceutical company that created the drug. Thus there is no true competition to force the price of the drug down. Consequently, while the prescription plan may pay a percentage of the cost, these drugs will usually have the highest out-of-pocket expense for the patient.

- *Older* **Name Brand Drugs**—as long as these drugs are still under patent protection and no other company can manufacture them, the company that created the drug can still charge a higher price for them. However, since they are not the newest drug used to treat a condition, the price for them is usually less than the cost of the first category of drugs. As a result, the patient will have a lower out-of-pocket expenditure.

- **Generic Drugs**—these are drugs that are no longer under patent protection. This means that any pharmaceutical company can manufacture a version of this drug. The resulting competition drives prices down. This will be the type of medication that is available under the $4 plans offered by some pharmacies. In fact, some drug stores also offer certain generic antibiotics at no cost.

## Over-the-Counter (OTC) Medications

Over-the-Counter (OTC) medications are the medicines that require no prescription. They can be purchased in any pharmacy. The number of OTC medications that are available and the conditions that they treat are far too numerous to list here. Oftentimes they are medications that were once available only by prescription, but over time they have been removed from the list of drugs that require that a doctor write a pre-scription for them.

## Tips for Saving Money on Prescriptions

- Mail order for prescriptions—check your prescription drug plan to determine if it offers a discount for purchasing medications through a preferred mail order firm.

- Buy prescriptions for more than one month at a time—a number of prescription drug plans offer a discount when prescriptions are ordered or purchased quarterly.

- Split pills—ask your doctor if the medication tablets you take can be prescribed in higher dosages and then split in half. This would provide a two-month supply of pills for the price of a single month. **NOTE: Many medications cannot be split without affecting their performance. Under *no* circumstances should a person do this without first obtaining the approval of the prescribing physician.**

- Sample packets—many times doctors are given sample packets of certain medications by the pharmaceutical company's sales representative whose job it is to promote the use of the company's medications. Ask your doctor if he or she can give you sample packs so that you can determine if the medication solves your medical problems *before* you spend money filling the prescription.

- Generic medication—always ask your doctor if there is a generic medication that can be used to treat your condition that will be as effective as the name brand that he or she was going to prescribe.

## Tips for Saving Money on OTC Medications

- Buying in bulk—when buying OTC medications, rather than buying two small bottles of a medication such as aspirin or antihistamines, buy a single large bottle with two to three times the number of pills as the smaller bottles. The large bottle will not cost two to three times as much as two or three bottles of the small one.

- Buy store brands—when buying OTC medications, remember that the generic store brand is frequently just as effective as the name brand. Buying generic typically saves a considerable amount of money over the course of a year.

- Coupons—more and more OTC medicines are offered for sale with discount coupons. The coupons *may* make the name brand less expensive than the generic store brand.

## CONCLUSION

Medical and dental insurance exists to help people pay the costs associated with maintaining wellness and treating ill health. As we've seen, these insurance plans come in various forms.

- Point of Service (POS) plans require that the patient pay for the office visit and/or treatment and then apply for reimbursement from the insurance company. This reimbursement is typically based on the "reasonable and customary" rates in the patient's geographic location.

- Preferred Provider Organization (PPO) plans have negotiated rates with physicians and dentists who then become part of a network of preferred providers. When the patient goes to an in-network provider, he or she will be responsible for only a relatively small co-payment portion of the bill.

- Health Maintenance Organization (HMO) plans generally operate their own facilities and the patient receives treatment from an employee of the organization. Again, this typically limits the patient's share of the bill to a relatively small co-payment.

The Children's Health Insurance Program (CHIP), started in 1997, provides low or no cost health care to children who meet certain financial guidelines. Each state administers its own CHIP.

Like medical insurance, dental insurance offers choices in the types of policies offered.

Coverage for prescription drugs will usually require a co-payment that is based on which of three categories the drug is in.

- New name brand drugs are covered but typically have the highest co-pay because they are under patent protection; they can be manufactured only by the company that created them.

- Older name brand drugs that have been available for a number of years but are still under patent protection usually have a co-payment that is less than the newest name brands, but that co-payment is also higher than the co-payment for generic drugs.

- Generic drugs are medications that are no longer under patent protection and can be manufactured by anyone. Generics typically have the lowest co-payment requirement.

When medication is prescribed, there are several ways to control the cost.

- If the medication must be taken on an ongoing basis, many insurance plans provide drug coverage that reduces costs by using mail-order services.

- Buy prescriptions for more than one more at a time.

- Split pills if, and only if, the doctor approves it.

- Manufacturers' representatives frequently provide physicians with free samples. Ask if the doctor can give you some so you can make certain that the medication works as expected before you spend money on it.

- A number of pharmacies offer generic medications at a significantly reduced price. Ask your doctor if one of those reduced cost medications can be used. Ask the physician if a generic is available.

When purchasing over-the-counter medications,

- Buy in bulk whenever it is feasible

- Use store brands

- Look for coupons in the mail, in newspapers, and on-line

You can control the cost of medical care. But to do so, you must be an active participant in the process.

## CHAPTER 11

# Retirement Planning

*Getting Ready for the Ultimate Level of Unemployment*

"When you retire, think and act as if you were still working; when you're still working, think and act a bit as if you were already retired."
— Author Unknown

At some point after obtaining a job, whether it's the first job or the last job, everyone dreams of the day when it is no longer necessary to get up every day and go to work. Unfortunately, dreaming of that day does not get us anywhere close to making that dream a reality. It takes hard work and four key ingredients:

- A plan

- Money

- A way to make the money grow

- Time for the money to work

The sooner money goes to work for you, the easier it is to accumulate enough to maintain a comfortable lifestyle in retirement.

## A Plan

The word *plan* is often used to describe a retirement vehicle; for example, a 401k *Plan*. For our purposes, let's use the word *plan* in a different context: a map that will lead to financial security in retirement. Funds do not instinctively migrate into some type of retirement instrument or vehicle. We, the wage earners, must have a plan for moving money out of our "everyday expenses budget" and into the vehicle that we have chosen to hold and grow that money for future use. This simply means we must make the commitment to deliberately find money and set it aside, acting as though we never had it.

> *Imagine for a moment that you live in a society where only cash is used. Every Friday, you get your pay in cash. You drive home and, every Friday, there is a lineup in your front yard of people you see regularly: the guy from the power company, the woman from the water company, another guy from the phone company, and so on.*

> *Every Friday, you get out of the car and start handing money out to the people in line. You pay cash for the electricity you used and cash for the water you used and cash for the garbage being collected. Everybody gets a share of your cash.*

> *Now, at the very end of the line is a little old man or a little old woman holding a teacup. You look into your wallet and find that there is just one dollar bill left, so you put it into the teacup.*

*The next week you go through the same ritual and, when the old man or old woman gets to the front of the line, you find that this week there are two dollar bills left, so you put them both into the teacup.*

*The next week you find that you're three dollars short, so you steal them out of the teacup.*

This scenario could continue all your life, but what's the point? The point is, who is the old man or old woman with the teacup? Have you figured it out yet?

The old man or old woman is *you* decades from now. You are literally standing last in line for your own money! Does this really make sense since you are the one who is working and earning it? The answer is a resounding "NO!"

What I'm suggesting here is that each of us goes to end of the line and grabs hold of the little old man or little old lady and drags our future self to the front of the line. Surprisingly, this person really doesn't want to be there and will fight—kicking and screaming—to stop from being put at the head of the line. But if you are strong enough to take control and insist on keeping your future self at the head of the line, you can announce to the world,

*"From now on, the old man and old woman get paid first. Then you guys can fight it out for the rest!"*

When you do this, the most amazing thing will happen. From that day forward, *everybody* gets paid instead of *everybody else* gets paid.

So, how can you make this happen? Where can you find this money?

- **Payroll Deductions**—one way to ensure that money is set aside every payday is to set up automatic payroll deductions. By developing a plan in which this happens, the money is moved before you ever "see" it, minimizing the chance that the money will be diverted to other purposes.

- **Automatic Deductions from Checking and Savings Accounts—** most banks will establish automatic deductions from checking accounts with the funds going into a savings account or an investment account. By making this the first transaction after every payday, you ensure that *you* get paid, too.

- **Build Savings into the Budget—**the overwhelming majority of people put savings into their budgets only when they've listed everything else that they can think of; savings is merely an afterthought. Instead, make it the first item built into your budget and be consistent about it.

## Money

Still looking for money to save? Ask this simple question:

*"Do I spend $2 per day that I could save if I wanted to?"*

Think about it—nearly everyone has some daily extra to save on. What do you have? Here are a few examples I've heard:

- *"I go out to lunch at a restaurant or fast food place every workday."*

- *"I buy snacks like chips and candy bars from vending machines at the office."*

- *"I drive on the toll roads even though I could take other routes for free."*

- *"I spend more than $2 a day on cigarettes."*

- *"I buy bottled water."* (This, rather than carrying a refillable bottle)

- *"I grab breakfast and coffee at convenience stores on my way to work."*

- *"I buy sodas whenever I'm driving."*

- *"I eat breakfast in the cafeteria at work instead of eating before I leave the house."*

- *"I could save money if I planned my errands more efficiently. I know it would save gas money along with wear and tear on my car, but I just don't get around to it."*

Can you identify with any of these statements? The sources of savings are nearly as numerous as the number of people looking for ways to save money. It's simply a matter of identifying those things that are less important than saving for your future. Each person makes those choices individually.

## A Way to Make Money Grow

Money saved and money invested will grow at different rates. Because saving usually involves low risk vehicles such as savings accounts and certificates of deposit, growth is slow because low risk yields low returns. Invested funds, however, offer greater opportunities for growth but carry a greater risk of loss. When the funds will be needed far into the future, greater risks are acceptable in order to have opportunities for greater returns. We'll examine investment opportunities at greater length shortly.

Perhaps of equal importance to investment opportunities is the tax classification of how the money is growing. Consider taxable growth versus tax deferred growth.

*Bruce and Sally each begin a program to accumulate money for retirement. Each has decided to save $2 a day rather than spend it. Each will receive an 8.00 percent annual rate of return. Both are in the 25 percent tax bracket.*

*Bruce has his money in a program where he will have to pay taxes on the money his program earns every year. At the end of 30 years, Bruce will have put $21,600 into the program; and, he will have $62,751 at the end of the 30-year period.*

*Sally has put her money into a program where the growth is tax deferred. She won't pay taxes on any of the program's earnings until she takes the money out of the program. She will have put $21,600 into the program; but, because the growth has not been taxed throughout the 30 years, she will have $78,084. Obviously, Sally will have to pay taxes on this money when she withdraws it. However, she will pay those taxes only as she withdraws it. Historically, most people are in a lower tax bracket after retirement than they were in while they were working.*

Clearly, tax deferred accumulation is far superior to taxable accumulation. Let's take a look at some programs that offer tax deferred growth. Many of the plans below use numbers in their names. Don't let these numbers intimidate you. The numbers simply identify the section of the Internal Revenue Code that authorizes the tax deferred growth of the money.

**Section 408—Traditional IRA**—a traditional IRA allows a person to set money aside every year for retirement. If the person is under age 50, he or she can contribute up to $5,000 per year. Wage earners age 50 and older can contribute up to $6,000 per year using the "catch-up" provision. Since tax law changes frequently, it is always a good idea to consult your tax professional when making retirement planning decisions.

Contributions may or may not be tax deductible. Deductibility is dependent on whether the taxpayer has access to a qualified retirement plan at his or her place of employment.

- If a qualified retirement plan is not available at work, the contribution will be fully deductible.

- If a qualified retirement plan is available at work (whether he or she contributes to the plan or not), the contributions will be fully deductible when the taxpayer has a Modified Adjusted Gross Income (MAGI) below a specific dollar amount.[12]

- If a qualified retirement plan is available at work (whether he or she contributes to it or not), the contributions will not be deductible if the taxpayer has a MAGI over the maximum.

Money in a Traditional IRA grows on a tax deferred basis. Simply stated, this means that the growth will not be taxed until it is withdrawn from the plan. When funds are withdrawn, they are taxed as ordinary income, and there are restrictions on withdrawal.

- If money is withdrawn from a Traditional IRA prior to age 59½, the taxpayer will pay ordinary income taxes on the money; *plus*, he or she will also pay a 10 percent penalty on the money that was withdrawn.

  - o There is one exception to the assessment of the penalty: if the money is paid out in substantially equal distributions for five years or until age 59½ (whichever is longer), the penalty is waived. An example would be a person

---

[12] The maximum MAGI can change from year to year. Always talk with a tax professional before making any decisions that could have tax consequences.

taking money out at the same rate every month or year (say, $1,000 per month).

- Withdrawals must begin by age 70½. The amount that must be withdrawn each year is known as the Required Minimum Distribution (RMD). The RMD is recalculated each year based on life expectancy at that year's age. The taxpayer who fails to take the RMD in any year will pay a penalty tax that is 50 percent of amount that was not withdrawn.

**Section 408a—ROTH IRA**—a Roth IRA is very much like a Traditional IRA. However, there are some significant differences between the two plans.

- First, the contributions are not tax deductible. All contributions are made using after-tax dollars.

- Second, the taxpayer can make the maximum allowable contribution until his or her maximum Modified Adjusted Gross Income exceeds a specific dollar amount set by the IRS.[13]

- Third, when the taxpayer begins taking distributions from the Roth IRA, all money withdrawn is received tax free, both principle and growth!

- Fourth, where withdrawals from a Traditional IRA prior to age 59½ are generally taxed and penalized, a Roth IRA permits withdrawals prior to age 59½ in specific situations. These situations include

    o The taxpayer has become disabled before attaining age 59½.

---

[13] The maximum MAGI can change from year to year. Always talk with a tax professional before making any decisions that could have tax consequences.

o The money withdrawn is used for a first-time home purchase.

o The money withdrawn is used to pay for post-secondary school expenses.

o The money withdrawn is used to pay for health insurance after a lengthy period of unemployment.

o The money withdrawn is used to pay catastrophic medical expenses.

o The taxpayer dies.

One additional dissimilarity must be noted here. Where the owner of a Traditional IRA must begin RMDs by age 70½, the owner of a Roth IRA is not required to take distributions at any time. If the taxpayer has no need of the money in the plan and chooses to leave the funds in the plan, he or she has the right to do so and the tax deferred growth continues.

**401k Plans**—these plans are designed specifically for employees of for-profit companies. Again, these plans and a Traditional IRA have a great many similarities. Both plans place untaxed money into a retirement plan. As with a Traditional IRA, there are certain limitations to the amount of money that can be contributed. And as with a Traditional IRA, the taxpayer will be taxed and penalized on any withdrawals made prior to attaining age 59½.

Unlike a Traditional IRA, money contributed to a 401k plan *must* be contributed by way of payroll deductions. The employee chooses how the funds will be invested by selecting specific investment vehicles from a list provided by the employer and the employer's plan administrator. Since the employee has the right to move the funds from one investment to another within the plan, the employee takes responsibility for the performance of the investments.

Just as with a Traditional IRA, required minimum distributions must begin by age 70½ and there are penalties for failing to take the RMD in any year.

**403b Plans**—while 401k plans are designed for employees of for-profit companies, 403b plans are specifically intended for the employees of 501(c)3 non-profit organizations, public school employees, the workers at cooperative hospital service organizations, certain ministers, and others. Just as with a 401k plan, contributions must be made via payroll deductions, but the maximum annual contribution limit is significantly higher than the limit on a 401k. Again as with a 401k plan or a Traditional IRA, the money grows tax deferred and is taxed as ordinary income at the time of withdrawal.

Withdrawals or Required Minimum Distributions must begin by age 70½. If funds are withdrawn prior to age 59½, the taxpayer will be required to pay ordinary income taxes and the same 10 percent penalty that is assessed on early withdrawals from a Traditional IRA or 401k plan.

**457 Plans**—finally, 457 deferred compensation plans are designed for employees of state and local governments along with employees of certain 501(c)3 non-profit organizations. Functionally, 403b and 457 plans have some similarities and some differences.

Similarities include the tax deferred growth of money inside the plan and required minimum distributions beginning no later than age 70½.

Differences include the obviously different workers to whom the plans are directed and the maximum allowable annual contributions into each plan.[14]

---

[14] Annual maximum contributions into each of these qualified retirement plans are subject to change annually as mandated by law. Always talk with your qualified tax professional to ensure that you do not exceed the maximum annual contribution limit.

## The Magic of Compound Interest and Time for Money to Work

**Compound Interest**—Albert Einstein is often credited with calling compound interest the "eighth wonder of the world." It is not certain that the eminent physicist actually said this, but the sentiment is certainly true. The difference between simple interest and compound interest is relatively easy to explain.

Simple interest is paid on the principle investment only. Compound interest, on the other hand, pays not only on the principle investment, but also on the already earned interest. To appreciate the potential implication on your bottom line, consider the following examples:

> Toby has $100 and puts it into an account that is earning 5 percent simple interest. At the end of the first year, his account is credited with $5 and his new balance is $105. At the end of the second year, he is again credited with $5 interest (based on the original principle) and his new balance is $110. At the end of the third year, another $5 interest is added to the account and he has a balance of $115.

> Sam also has $100 to invest. He places it into an account that is earning 5 percent compound interest. At the end of the first year, his account is credited with $5 and his new balance is $105. At the end of the second year, he is credited with $5.25 interest (5 percent of $105, the new principle) and his new balance is $110.25. At the end of the third year, he is credited with 5 percent interest on the $110.25 and he has a balance of $115.76.

While the difference in balances may seem insignificant in this example, it becomes much more pronounced when more money is involved over a longer period of time.

**The Benefit of Time**—time is the second "magic ingredient" when saving money for a future goal. The longer the period of time during which money is put to work, the larger will be the outcome. If a person wants to know how long it will take money to double, apply the Rule of 72.

The Rule of 72 states that one simply divides the number 72 by the interest rate. The result of this calculation will tell the number of years it will take the money to double. For example, if an account is earning 6 percent compound interest, it will double every twelve years (72/6 = 12). Alternatively, if the account is earning 12 percent interest, the money will double every six years.

Now, to fully appreciate the combination of time and compound interest, let's look at this long-term example.[15]

> Ryan has decided to set aside $100 every month on the first day of the month. His investment account will earn a continuous 5 percent for the entire time that the account exists.
>
> At the end of ten years Ryan has invested a total of $12,000, and this investment has grown to $15,758.
>
> He continues to invest $100 each month so that, at the end of twenty years, his actual investment has grown to $24,000. Now his balance is $41,546.
>
> For the third decade, he continues his $100 per month investment so that his total investment at the end of thirty years is $36,000. But now, thanks to the magic of compound interest and time, his account is worth $84,019.

---

[15] The results shown in this example are purely for illustrative purposes. The illustration is hypothetical and does not represent the actual returns on any specific investment or investment program.

The graph below clearly illustrates the value of both time and compound interest.

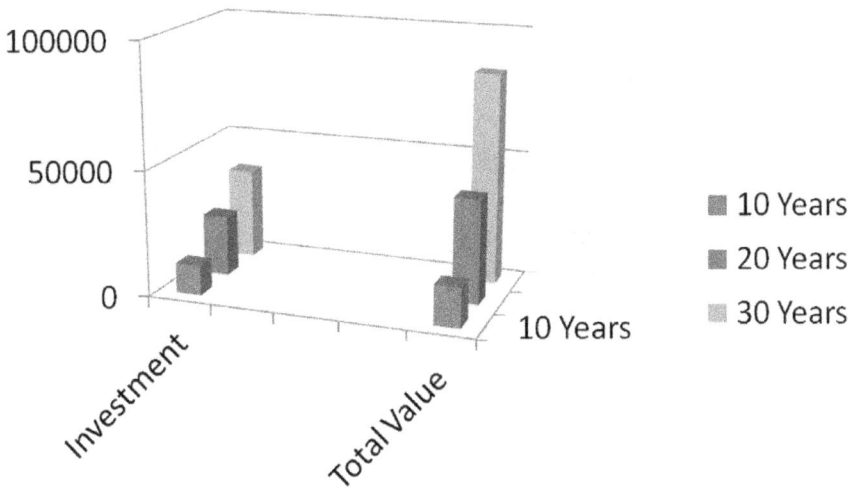

FIGURE 11.1

## Terminology

Before discussing where money can be invested, it is best to ensure that everyone is using the same terminology to mean the same things. Here are some terms you should be familiar with:

- **Savings Account**—this is a traditional savings account at a bank. Money is deposited and is credited with interest over time. The account owner can add money to the account at any time and withdraw funds at any time.

- **Certificate of Deposit (aka CD)**—this is essentially a savings account with a commitment that the money will be left in the account for a specific period of time. In return for promising not to withdraw money from the account before the expiration of the CD, the account owner is promised an interest rate that is usually higher than the interest being paid on a traditional savings account. Money cannot be added to the account during the time that the money is committed for; and, if money is withdrawn from the account before the commitment time has passed, the account owner will be penalized a portion of the interest that was promised. CDs have typical durations of three months to five years.

- **Annuity**—an annuity is a contract purchased from an insurance company. When the annuity is purchased, the investor can invest a single lump sum of money into the contract. If the annuity is a fixed annuity, the contract will pay interest on the money in the account based on the investment returns earned by the insurance company. A fixed annuity cannot lose value.

  If the person has purchased a variable annuity, the policy owner will select the investments into which the money will be placed and a return on investment will be credited to the account. If the investments make money, the balance in the annuity goes up. If the investments lose money, the balance in the annuity goes down.

  An indexed annuity puts the money into a "basket" of stocks or bonds or some other investment index. The growth or decline of the value of the account balance will be determined by the positive or negative performance of the index.

- **Stock**—stock represents an ownership interest in a company. For example, if the Acme Corporation has sold 100 shares of stock and John owns 10 shares, John is a 10 percent owner of the company. As an owner, John is entitled to a share of the profits and will receive a *dividend* that represents 10 percent of the profit that is distributed to the owners.

- **Bond**—where stock represents an ownership interest, a bond represents money that has been loaned to a borrower. If John has purchased a $1,000 bond from the Acme Corporation, he has loaned that money to the company. If John buys a U.S. Government Bond, he has loaned money to the federal government. Interest may be paid throughout the duration of the loan, or it may be paid when the bond matures (i.e., when the loan must be fully repaid).

- **Mutual Funds**—when people do not have the time to manage their own investments, or when they do not feel that they have the knowledge and/or expertise to manage their own investments, they may choose to purchase mutual funds. Essentially, this is an investment in which a group of people who all have the same investment goals and philosophies have hired a professional money manager to manage the investments for them. Mutual funds may invest in stocks, bonds, or both depending on the investment objective and philosophy of the fund.

- **Real Estate Investment Trust (REIT)**—somewhat like a mutual fund, an REIT's manager buys properties and manages them for the benefit of the owners of the REIT. Depending on the objectives and philosophy of the REIT, the manager may buy shopping centers, apartments, office buildings, or other types of property. If the value of a piece of property owned by the REIT goes up, the value of each REIT share goes up. If the value of the property goes down, the value of each share goes down. If the property rents out space to tenants, the property value goes up when occupancy is full but goes down if there is unrented, vacant space. REITs often have minimum investment requirements that are higher than the minimums for some mutual funds, stocks, or bonds.

- **Risk**—people buy investments in the anticipation of gain: making money. However, risk acknowledges the possibility that money can be lost. There are different kinds of risk.

o   Market risk is the possibility that there will not be a buyer when an owner wants to sell, or that the potential buyer is not willing to pay the price that the seller is asking for.

o   Inflation risk is the possibility that when an investment is sold, the money will have less buying power than the original money invested had. Think about how many bags of groceries could be filled by spending $20.00 twenty years ago, and compare it to how many bags can be filled today—*that* is inflation risk.

o   Default risk is the possibility that a borrower will not be able to repay a debt.

o   Opportunity risk is the possibility that a person will not be able to take advantage of an opportunity because his or her cash is tied up in some other endeavor.

o   Interest rate risk is the possibility that you may have loaned money at a specific rate of interest only to have the demand for loans, and consequently interest rates, go up while your money is tied up in a lower interest rate loan.

This is only a small sampling of the various risks that confront us every day, often without our even recognizing the existence of the risk.

## Where Do I Invest This Money?[16]

Perhaps as never before, people have many options for the saving and investing of their money. The sheer number of available options can feel overwhelming to the point that a person may be paralyzed into

---

[16] The information here does not constitute specific recommendations for any individual or group of individuals. Always seek the assistance of a qualified financial advisor before making investment decisions.

*inaction,* much like the proverbial deer in the headlights. To offer a bit of clarification, let's start by determining when the money will be needed—in the near term or at some distant time in the future.

**Short-Term**—money that will be needed in the near term should not be placed into investments that carry the risk of loss of capital. For example, a parent who will need a specific amount of money to pay college tuition for a child in the fall cannot take the risk that the investment will lose money. There simply is not enough time to recover lost capital. The funds should be placed into a low risk/no risk investment. Examples include savings accounts and short-term certificates of deposit at a bank. The investments will pay low rates of return (interest) because these instruments are guaranteed not to lose value.

**Intermediate-Term**—funds needed in the intermediate term will not be required immediately. They may have time horizons of anywhere between two years from today and ten years down the road. Examples of investments suited for this time frame might include longer duration certificates of deposit, short-term bond mutual funds, and some high quality stocks.

**Long-Term**—while definitions vary, most people tend to think of anything longer than ten years as a long-term proposition. The true objective of long-term investments is to have the money grow faster than the rate of inflation so that the money has greater purchasing power than it originally had. Stocks, bonds, mutual funds, annuities, and REITs all tend to be thought of as long-term investments.

Retirement planning is great example of a long-term investment program. When a person is young and has many years until retirement, it is acceptable to take higher risks because there is "plenty of time" to recover from a loss. However, as one gets older, risk management requires reducing exposure to the risk of loss.

One last note on retirement planning: when companies offer self-directed retirement plans such as 401ks, 403bs, SIMPLE IRAs, and the like, they have a responsibility under Section 404c of The Employee Retirement

Income Security Act (ERISA) of 1974 to provide their employees with sufficient information for the employees to make well informed investment decisions within their plan. If your company offers such a plan, ask what information it makes available and if they have competent investment advisors come into the workplace to educate employees about their options and answer questions that the workers may have.

## CONCLUSION

Because few individuals today will work for the same company throughout their working lifetime, and because few employers today offer a traditional pension plan that pays retirees a monthly stipend based on their years of employment, it takes hard work and planning to make the dream of a comfortable retirement come true. Saving for the future never has happened and never will happen by itself.

To plan for a comfortable retirement, there are several necessary ingredients.

- A plan

- Money

- A way to make money grow

    o Individual Retirement Accounts (IRA)

    o Roth IRAs

    o Employer plans

        ➢ 401(k) programs

        ➢ 403(b) plans

        ➢ 457 plans

> ➢ Many others

- Time

  o When the miracle of compound interest is given time to work, the results can be amazing. The more years over which interest is allowed to compound, the more likely a person is to like the outcome.

Knowing the terminology of retirement planning empowers investors to clearly communicate the types of investments with which they are comfortable.

- Savings accounts

- Certificate of deposit

- Annuity

- Stock

- Bond

- Mutual fund

- Real Estate Investment Trust

The concept of risk is going to affect where and how we invest our money; and, it should be noted here that there are different kinds of risks. To name just a few, there are

- Market Risk

- Inflation Risk

- Default Risk

- Opportunity Risk

- Interest Rate Risk

An old banker's adage tells us that reward follows risk and risk follows reward. The greater the risks we accept, the greater the possibility for larger gains or larger losses. The less risk the greater the probability that we will obtain smaller gains or endure smaller losses.

Where we invest our retirement funds will be dependent on the risks we are willing to take.

- Banks offer

    o   Savings accounts

    o   Certificates of deposit

- Insurance companies offer annuities

- Brokerages offer

    o   Stocks

    o   Bonds

    o   Mutual Funds

    o   Real Estate Investment Trusts (REIT)

The time frame in which we want our dream to come true will also determine the risks we take and where we can invest our funds

- When the time frame is short (perhaps one to two years), protection of principle (i.e., safety) becomes very important.

- When the time frame is an intermediate term (say, two to ten years), prudent risks may be acceptable as there is time for the plan to recover from a financial setback.

- Long-term (greater than ten years), higher levels of risk are acceptable, again because the plan has time to recover from a financial setback.

It has long been said that the only difference between a retired gentleman and an old man is money—the money to do the things he's dreamed of doing in his golden years. The same is true for ladies. Planning for retirement is not something that can be delegated to someone else. Your financial future is in your hands.

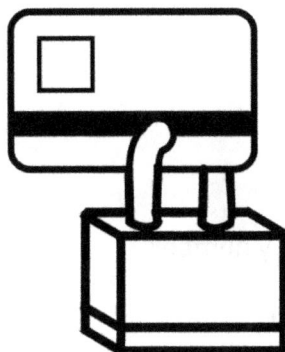

## CHAPTER 12

# Preventing Identity Theft

*Someone's Using My Good Name for a Bad Purpose!*

"The measure of a man's real character is what he would do if he knew he never would be found out."

— Thomas Babington Macaulay

Don't look now, but someone may have already targeted you for a robbery. This thief won't need a gun or a knife to rob you; all this thief needs is a little bit of information about you.

It's called *identity theft,* and it's one of the fastest growing white collar crimes in the country. In fact, a study done by Javelin Strategy and Research estimated that 1 in every 10 U.S. consumers has been the victim of identity thieves. Interestingly, 7 percent of *these* victims had their identity stolen for the purpose of committing medical fraud.

Identity thieves want information about you; the more the better! They want to know things like

- Your name

- Your address

- Your birth date

- Your social security number

- Your bank account number

- Your credit card account numbers

- Your account passwords

- Any other financial information that they can get

## Where Do Thieves Get This Information?

**Dumpster Diving**—perhaps one of the most thoroughly mined sources of information is your trash. Anything that contains personal information about you that you throw away is an identity thief's pot of gold at the end of the rainbow.

**Skimming**—you give your credit card to the server at a restaurant or to the clerk at the store and they run it through twice saying it didn't read the card the first time. There is a good chance that the first run was a skimmer that reads and records information from your card. The second time was when the charge was actually recorded. Thanks to the skimmer, the identity thief has all of the information about that credit account and can begin using it to either make charges for himself or herself, or can use that account information as a reference to begin opening new accounts that you will never know about until a collection agent calls you. The thief can also sell your information to another thief.

Another form of skimming involves miniature transmitter chips known as RFID (Radio Frequency Identification) tags that have been installed in thousands of credit and debit cards. Touted by credit card companies as a convenience that will speed the card owner through the checkout counter, these RFID tags send the account information to a receiver that captures the account data and records the purchase. The problem is that a person who passes near you can also capture all of your account information with a small and inexpensive portable receiver concealed in a purse or briefcase. Once the thief has this information, it can be used to make unauthorized purchases and to establish new lines of credit.

**Changing Addresses**—the identity thief files a change of address card at the post office with your name and a false address. The thief now gets all of your mail including statements on your current accounts with all of the account information on them, and all of those fabulous "Congratulations, you're pre-approved for this credit card" letters. The thief simply fills out the application using your name and the false address and, *voila*, one new account that the thief can use to charge purchases and you are none the wiser...until you are denied credit due to a poor payment history, or a collection agent calls.

**Stealing**—you're on vacation, walking down a busy street. A man or woman bumps into you, apologizes, and walks on. You think nothing of it until you reach for your wallet and find that it is gone, along with your driver's license, credit cards, social security card, and a wealth of other information that allows the identity thief to impersonate you.

**Pretexting**—the identity thief contacts you claiming to be someone or something he or she is not. Perhaps one caller is conducting a survey; another claims to be a representative of someone you customarily do business with. The thief simply asks you to verify some information. Some of it is correct and some of it is wrong until you correct it for the thief. You now have a financial clone who is using your good name for a bad purpose.

**Hacking**—who says you can't conjure up an identity out of thin air? An identity thief sits in a parked car in front of the house and hacks into your unsecured home wireless network, reading your mail, viewing your electronic account statements, everything!

**Phishing**—this is a "fishing expedition" for your private information and can be conducted in a variety of ways. The phisher uses trickery and deception in order to persuade you to give him or her information that should not be given to someone you don't know. One way is the fake telephone survey like the one described under pretexting. Another way is to send an e-mail to you purporting to be someone or something else and asking that you either provide certain information or confirm certain information. Often the e-mail bears the logo of your bank or stock broker's firm, and the logo looks real—so real that security specialists often have trouble distinguishing the real logo from the fake one.

Take a look at a crude example of phishing. This is an e-mail I actually received in my e-mail at work!

## EFTPS                                    ONLINE
THE EAISEST WAY TO PAY YOUR **FEEDRAL** TAXES

Your Federal Tax Payment **ID: 01037594728** has been not accepted.

---

**Pelase**, make sure that all **inforamtion** you have **submtited** is **corerct** and refer to Code R21 to find out the **infromation** about **comapny payemnt**. **Plaese conatct** this page if you have any questions: http://eftps.gov/R21

**Rteurn** Reason Code R21 - The **idetnification nmuber** you **entreed** in the **Comapny Idetnification Feild** is not functional. Try **sedning ifnormation** to your **accuontant avdiser** using other **otpions.**

# EFTPS: The Electronic Federal Tax Payment System

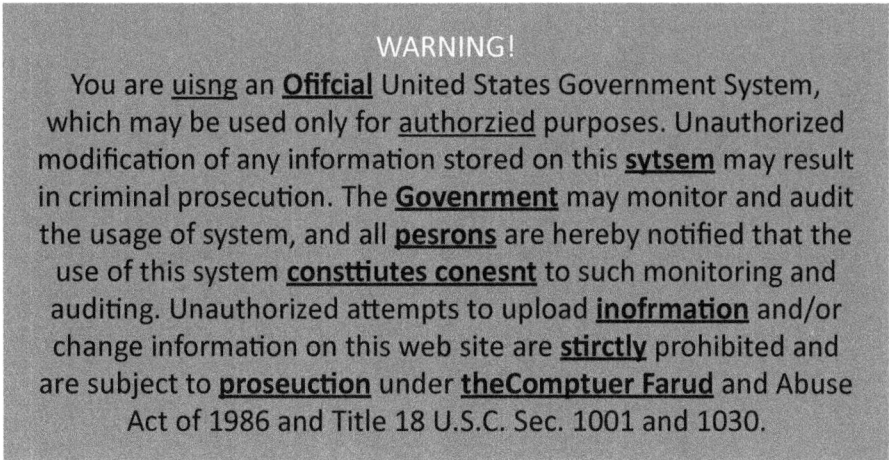

> **WARNING!**
> You are <u>uisng</u> an **Ofifcial** United States Government System, which may be used only for <u>authorzied</u> purposes. Unauthorized modification of any information stored on this **sytsem** may result in criminal prosecution. The **Govenrment** may monitor and audit the usage of system, and all **pesrons** are hereby notified that the use of this system **consttiutes conesnt** to such monitoring and auditing. Unauthorized attempts to upload **inofrmation** and/or change information on this web site are **stirctly** prohibited and are subject to **proseuction** under **theComptuer Farud** and Abuse Act of 1986 and Title 18 U.S.C. Sec. 1001 and 1030.

FIGURE 12.1

This phisherman has done a few things to make this look like the real deal and lots of things that clearly mark this as a rough attempt to gain information.

- What Makes It Look Real

    o  Sent out at income tax time, this phishing e-mail plays on taxpayers' fears of having something go wrong with their tax filing and the possibility of an audit.

    o  With more and more taxpayers filing and paying on-line, the thief has used an acronym (what government agency doesn't have its own version of alphabet soup?) and purports to be from the Electronic Federal Tax Payment System (EFTPS), a real entity.

    o  Even the WARNING! in Figure 12.1 (stating that this is an official United States Government System and citing the Computer Fraud and Abuse Act of 1986 and Title 18 U.S.C. Sec. 1001 and 1030) makes it look very official and very ominous. FYI: Title 18 U.S.C. Sec. 1030 really *does* address the issue of hacking into federal government computers and computers belonging to certain financial institutions!

- Tip-Offs That It's Not Real

    o The spelling and grammar are terrible. All of the under-lines point out misspelled words. However, the origi-nal text of the message did not have all the misspelled words bolded and underlined. The reader had to read the message carefully to realize the number of mistakes it contained.

It's all very ugly, and it's sad how many people fall prey to tricks like this every year.

## What to Do If Your Identity Is Stolen

1. Immediately file a police report. The report number will be the first thing that any creditor or credit reporting agency will ask for when you contact them about the theft. They may ask you to send a copy of the report.

2. Notify all three credit reporting bureaus and ask that they put a fraud alert on your credit report. This alert is like a giant red flag on your credit report that tells prospective creditors that your identity has been stolen and that they should not open new accounts until they have obtained definitive proof that the real *you* is opening the account.

3. Notify the Federal Trade Commission of the theft. This agency of the federal government is charged with the responsibility of fight-ing identity theft. You can report the theft of your identity at

    http://www.ftc.gov/bcp/edu/microsites/idtheft/consumers/ filing-a-report.html

4.  Close all accounts that have been tampered with.

5.  Closely monitor your credit reports. Watch for

    - new accounts that you know nothing about

    - new addresses appearing on the report that could indicate statements for accounts are going to someone other than you

    - new inquiries by creditors who have been asked to open new accounts

    - new employers

    - the appearance of public records such as judgments for unpaid bills or bankruptcy filings

## Preventing Identity Theft

The really good news is that there are steps you can take to prevent the theft of your personal information. These steps include the following:

- If your credit or debit cards have an RFID tag, it may have the words "paypass," "paywave," or "blink" on it. It may have a symbol appearing like a series of half parentheses so that it looks like this:)))), or another symbol that your bank has created. If you have such a card, you can ask that the card issuer provide you with a new one that does *not* have an RFID tag in it; or you can wrap the card in aluminum foil before putting it in your wallet. This will prevent the chip from transmitting the information to fixed or portable scanner.

- Shred documents that contain information that an identity thief would want before throwing the documents away.

- Protect your social security number. While the card clearly states that it is not to be used for identity purposes, we all know how many places use it for exactly that purpose.

- Know whom you're really dealing with before releasing personal information.

- Don't use "obvious" passwords like a child's name, a pet's name, your birth date, or your anniversary. Instead, make passwords difficult to guess by using a combination of upper and lower case letters, add in numbers, and include symbols such as # or $ or &.

- Keep information secure. This includes not keeping your password "cheat sheet" on the bottom of your keyboard.

- Actively monitor your credit for all of the items listed above.

- Know when you *should* get a bill from a merchant or creditor, and be proactive when you don't get it. It may have been stolen out of your mailbox by an identity thief.

## Where to Get Your Credit Report

Federal law now allows you to obtain a copy of your credit report from each bureau annually at no cost. The website annualcreditreport.com was created to provide access to these reports and is sponsored by all three of the reporting bureaus. This website is not to be confused with numerous other websites that offer free credit reports with the intent of selling a monthly credit monitoring service. You will not get your credit score with your free report from these entities; however, the *bureaus* do offer to provide a score for a fee.

If you do not have access to the Internet, you can contact

Annual Credit Report Request Service
P.O. Box 105281
Atlanta, GA 30348-5281

You can also obtain a copy of each bureau's report by contacting the bureau directly. Here are the addresses for the three bureaus:

| Equifax | Experian | TransUnion |
|---|---|---|
| P.O. Box 740241 | P.O. Box 2002 | P.O. Box 1000 |
| Atlanta, GA 30374 | Allen, TX 75013 | Chester, PA 19022 |
| 800-685-1111 | 888-397-3742 | 800-888-4213 |
| www.equifax.com | www.experian.com | www.transunion.com |

## Where to Get More Information

Identity theft is constantly evolving and the tools to combat it are always undergoing change. To find additional information on this subject, try the following:

- www.ftc.gov/idtheft—this website is operated by the Federal Trade Commission and offers a tremendous amount of information about how to prevent identity theft, what to do if you are a victim of identity theft, tools for combating it, and much more.

- www.idtheftcenter.org—sponsored by the U.S. Department of Justice Office for Victims of Crimes, the California Consumer Protection Foundation, and many others, this website contains a wealth of information including state resources for combating identity theft and contact information for those resources.

- www.irs.gov—the official IRS website offers information regarding identity theft and tax records and what to do if the IRS contacts you regarding a tax issue that you believe may have been caused by identity theft.

- www.privacyrights.org—this non-profit organization provides resource information for a wide variety of privacy related issues including identity theft, debt collections, medical privacy, and much more.

- Call 877-IDTHEFT (877-437-4337)—also operated by the FTC, this is a resource center for those who do not have access to the internet.

- Write to the Identity Theft Clearing House, Federal Trade Commission, 600 Pennsylvania Avenue NW, Washington, D.C. 20580.

- Use your favorite search engine to research the subject of identity theft.

## CONCLUSION

Identity theft, the stealing of other people's personal, non-public information for the purpose of impersonating them, is one of the fastest growing white collar crimes today. All the identity thief needs is information, and that information can be gleaned from a variety of sources.

- Dumpster diving—stealing trash containing the information

- Skimming—scanning your credit card with a reader that stores the information on the card

- Changing your address—in order to intercept mail

- Stealing—your wallet, your credit cards, your mail

- Pretexting—pretending to be someone else to whom you would give this information

- Hacking—breaking into your computer's wireless network to capture information stored on your computer

- Phishing—the use of trickery or deception to obtain identifying information

When you believe that your identity has been stolen, take the following steps:

- File a police report

- Notify all three credit reporting bureaus and place a fraud alert on each report

- Notify the Federal Trade Commission

- Close any and all accounts that you believe the identity thief may have access to

- Closely monitor your credit report for any new accounts or unexplained credit activity

The good news is that there are steps you can take to protect yourself against identity theft

- Contact the credit card issuer and request that a new card be issued without the RFID chip; or wrap the card in aluminum foil to prevent the card from sending information to a scanner.

- Shred documents that contain identifying information before you throw them away.

- Protect your social security number; do not give it to unknown persons.

- Know whom you are dealing with before providing any identifying information.

- Avoid simple and easily guessed passwords; make them complex by combining upper and lower case letters with numbers and symbols.

- Keep password information secure.

- Monitor your credit report on a regular basis and take immediate actions if something appears to be wrong.

- Pay attention to see that bills arrive on time.

In order to monitor your credit reports, you can obtain them directly from the credit reporting bureaus. You will be charged for these reports. Alternatively, you can obtain the reports, though not your credit score, one time every 12 months at no cost through the website annualcreditreport.com.

## CHAPTER 13

# Credit Scores and Reports

*Since They Affect Our Lives in So Many Ways*
*It Might Be a Good Idea to Make Sure That They're Telling the Truth*

"Creditors have better memories than debtors."

— Benjamin Franklin

Anyone who has borrowed money has a credit history that can be found in a credit report. This report tells the good, the bad, and the *everything* about how a person pays his or her debts; and the report and its score affect many aspects of every person's life—often in ways that are not expected.

## What Is Affected by Credit History

**The Cost of Credit**—as a general rule, high credit scores usually mean that credit is available and that it is available at reasonable costs—that is, lower interest rates. When credit scores are low, interest rates on loans will be higher, *if* the loan is approved. Often, low credit scores result in the denial of credit.

**Your Job Search**—a significant number of potential employers are obtaining credit reports as part of their employment screening process. The logic behind this process is that how a person manages responsibilities in his or her personal life is indicative of how that person will manage professional responsibilities.

Of course, the prospective employer must have a valid, employment-related reason for requiring a credit report as part of the screening for a job. For example, if John is applying for a job mowing grass, there would not appear to be a reason for reviewing his credit history. However, if John is applying for a job in which he will be expected to handle other people's money, there is every reason to want a credit report review to ensure that John takes money management seriously.

Furthermore, the prospective employer must be consistent in the practice of using credit report reviews when screening applicants for a specific job. If John and Mary are both applying for the same position, the employer must review both individuals' credit report, or it should not review either.

The prospective employer must also obtain the applicant's permission to get a credit report. This permission is usually contained in the paragraph(s) immediately above where the applicant signs the job application. While the applicant has the right to withhold permission to obtain a credit report, the employer then has the right to not consider the individual's job application.

**The Cost of Insurance**—a little known fact, which we discussed in Chapter 8, is that credit scores often impact the price someone pays for insurance, specifically, auto insurance. While some insurance companies use this as just one of several factors in determining the price paid for the insurance, other companies use it as the *only* factor.

## How a Credit Score Is Created

### The Fair Isaac Company (FICO)

Credit scores based on models created by the Fair Isaac Company, now known as FICO, are based on five factors.

- A person's **payment history** accounts for approximately 35 percent of the credit score. Pay debts on time, as agreed, and credit scores rise. Pay debts late or don't make the required payments, and credit scores decline. Also included in this part of the score is the presence of adverse public records, such as bankruptcies, liens, collections, and the number of accounts that are past due.

- The **amount of money owed in relation to the amount of credit available** accounts for approximately 30 percent of the credit score. Run account balances up to the maximum, and credit scores decrease. Pay balances down so that only a small percentage of the available credit is owed, and credit scores tend to increase.

- The **number of years an account has been open** accounts for about 15 percent of the credit score. The longer an account has been open, the greater impact it will have on the score. A long history of timely payments has a very positive impact on the credit score. A long history of late payments or missed payments will have a greater negative impact.

- The **types of credit** used account for approximately 10 percent of the score. Are account balances all credit card debt; or is the amount owed a diverse mixture of both secured and unsecured debts? A diverse mix would include credit cards, retail store accounts, installment loans (e.g., auto loans), and mortgage loans.

- Finally, **recently opened accounts** account for about 10 percent of the score. Because new accounts do not have a "track record" that can be examined for behavioral patterns, new accounts tend to lower credit scores.

FICO Scores are frequently used by mortgage, auto, and other commercial lenders.

## Vantage Score

Alternatively, many vendors who sell credit scores, including some of the reporting bureaus, offer a new scoring system called "Vantage" to consumers who want to know their score. Unfortunately, since Vantage scores and FICO Scores are calculated in different ways, consumers can be confused by what they perceive to be inconsistencies. While five factors make up the FICO Score, six factors make up the Vantage score, and the factors are not weighted the same by the two systems.

- **Payment history** accounts for about 32 percent of the score.

- The **amount of credit currently in use** accounts for approximately 23 percent of the score.

- **Credit balances** account for about 15 percent of the score.

- The **kinds of credit** and the **age of the accounts** account for approximately 13 percent of the score.

- **New credit accounts** and **inquiries** account for 10 percent of the score.

- **Total available credit** accounts for 7 percent of the Vantage score.

The confusion between the two scores arises because of the differences between the minimum and maximum numbers used in each score. Consider this comparison:

|  | FICO | Vantage |
|---|---|---|
| Lowest Score | 300 | 501 |
| Highest Score | 850 | 990 |
| Mid-Point Score | 575 | 745 |

A consumer who is contemplating borrowing money may want to know his or her credit score before making the application in order to make an estimate of the interest rate. Obviously, it will be essential to know which score he or she is looking at. Since most lenders use FICO Scores when determining a person's credit worthiness, a consumer who has gotten a Vantage score will have an unrealistic opinion of his or her credit worthiness.

A free FICO Score Estimator is available at www.bankrate.com. Consumers can use this estimator to get an approximation of their current FICO Scores. When using this tool, remember that it is an estimate and does not guarantee that credit will be offered based on this estimate.

## "Good" Credit Scores

Here are general, though not universal valuations of FICO Scores:

- Between 700 and 760 and above—very good to excellent

- Below 700—only "fair"

At a point determined by each lender, a score will be below the acceptable minimum for offering credit.

Vantage scores use a grading scale similar to the one we all learned as children in school.

- 900 to 990 is an "A"

- 800 to 899 is a "B"

- 700 to 799 is a "C"

- 600 to 699 is a "D"

- 501 to 599 is an "F"

As with creditors using FICO scores, any creditor using Vantage scores has its own standard of an acceptable score and a score that is too low to offer credit.

## How to Establish "Good" Credit

Since everyone's payment history accounts for the largest percentage of the credit score, it is obvious that paying bills on time is probably the most significant thing a person can do to establish a good credit score, or raise one that is lower than desired.

Keep balances below 50 percent of credit limits.

If a payment is past due, it is important to bring the payment up to date as quickly as possible. Consider the plight of "Poor Peter" below, and it is easy to see why he is having trouble raising his credit score.

> *"Poor Peter" ran into a problem right after the holidays and missed his January payment to the Pecos River Department Store. When he made the minimum payment in February, he thought he'd brought the account up to date. But, in reality, he had made his January payment and was still 30 days past due.*

Until he makes two payments (for example, he could make a payment on March 10 and designate it as his February payment, and another payment on March 11 designating it as his March payment), he will continue to be 30 days past due.

Another practice to establish and maintain good credit is to keep outstanding balances below 50 percent of the available credit limit. As listed above, this is the second largest component of the FICO Score, and warrants appropriate attention.

When accounts are not used for a prolonged period of time, credit card companies have begun closing them. Since the closing of an account reduces the available credit, a closed account lowers a person's credit score. For this reason, it is important to periodically use the credit account so that it remains active; however, never charge more to the account than can be paid in full by the due date.

If accounts have been sent to collections, the best thing to do is to resolve the debt as quickly as possible. While paying the debt will not remove its record from the credit report, doing so will lessen the negative impact of the account on the credit score; and the further into the past it recedes, the less impact it will have.

## What to Do When Credit Is Damaged

When a credit score has been damaged, the first priority is to pay off the debts. This can be done in any of several ways.

- The first way is to **pay the debt in full**, immediately. This is most appropriate when the debt owed is small (has a low balance). Believe it or not, I've actually seen credit reports with old debts with a balance *under* $10! When the debt is small, pay it, get a receipt, and be done with it. Of course, not all debts have small balances. It may seem impractical to consider paying these larger debts with a single payment, but is it?

- The second way to resolve the debt is to **settle it for less than the full amount owed**. This is often the most practical choice when the original creditor has sold the debt to a third party collection agency. Consider this example:

*Four years ago, David bought a car and financed it through the Ninth National Bank. When he lost his job a year later, the car was repossessed and the lender sold the car at auction for $9,000. Because David still owed $13,000 on the car, the bank obtained a deficiency judgment for the remaining $4,000 and attempted to collect it from David.*

*Eighteen months later, Ninth National Bank sold the $4,000 IOU to the collection agency of Clawback and Pillager. As David's creditor, C&P can charge him interest at whatever rate the law allows. Now, a year after C&P bought the IOU, the debt has grown to $5,000.*

*Because C&P paid Ninth National Bank only $1,500 for the IOU, they do not need to collect the full balance to make a profit on the transaction. Consequently, a decision is made that the debt is eligible for settlement.*

*If David will give C&P $2,500, C&P will consider the debt to be paid and no further money will be owed to them.*

The advantages to both parties are obvious; C&P has made a 66 percent return on its initial investment, and David has paid off his debt for 50 cents on the dollar. What is not so obvious, from David's perspective, are the disadvantages/drawbacks/negative implications/consequences of settling the debt.

The first disadvantage is that C&P will probably report to the credit bureau that the debt was "settled in full" rather than "paid in full." This *might* affect David's ability to get credit in the future. While some creditors do not care how the debtor got the balance owed to zero, others care very much. Think of it this way: if I owe you money and pay you only half of it, how willing will you be to loan me money in the future?

The second disadvantage may be a surprise, and of huge immediate concern. It is that the Internal Revenue Service has determined that the money that David did not have to pay C&P is *taxable income* that David must report on his tax return for the year in which the debt is resolved.

When a debtor is offered a settlement, it may be a very viable and practical solution to the debt problem. However, the person who owes the money *must* examine both the advantages and disadvantages of all possible solutions; then, choose the solution that is best suited to that person's individual needs.

- The third solution is to seek the help of a non-profit credit counseling agency and enroll in a debt management program.

## Get Help

When a person is struggling with debt issues, it is best to seek the assistance of a legitimate credit counseling agency. Credit counseling agencies can often intercede with the creditors to obtain concessions that will help a person pay the debts off, in full, over a period of time. The concessions may include the following:

- Re-aging of accounts, which could mean the cessation of late fees and/or overlimit fees

- Lower monthly payments so that payments are easier to budget for

- Reduced interest rates so that more of every payment is applied to the debt rather than just to the interest

When selecting a credit counseling agency, key factors to look for are

- A non-profit agency that qualifies for a 501(c)3 tax status from the IRS—while many agencies may purport to be "not for profit," they have adopted a business model that is designed to generate significant income for themselves and their for profit affiliates. A 501(c)3 designation indicates that the Internal Revenue Service has determined that the agency exists primarily for a charitable purpose. A charitable purpose includes the provision of *education* to the public. As a charitable organization, the agency is exempted from paying federal income taxes and must operate for the charitable purpose (or purposes) for which it was established. Failure to adhere to these requirements will result in the revocation of the agency's tax exempt status.

- Counselors who have been certified by a reputable third party—this does not mean that the agency creates its own counselor training program. Rather it means that the counselors must pass a certification course developed and administered by an independent organization, one that is not controlled by the agency.

- Membership in the National Foundation for Credit Counseling—as the premier organization for credit counseling agencies, the NFCC has set several criteria, including high standards for the quality of counseling delivered, the financial stability of the counseling agency, and the ethical treatment of clients. A full audit of the agency's financial management is required annually to ensure that the funds received from donors are properly administered for the attainment of the agency's charitable purpose, and that client funds are segregated from the agency's operating funds and disbursed promptly to the client's creditors.

- Accreditation by the Council on Accreditation (COA)—accreditation by the COA is a long and expensive process in which this independent third party inspects and verifies that policies and procedures are in place and adhered to by the agency for the protection of its clients. By choosing to undergo this accreditation process, the agency demonstrates its commitment to transparency and doing what is best for its clients.

- A Board of Directors comprised of independent parties who take seriously their responsibility for the oversight of the agency's management and operations—the Board should have members who are respected leaders in their communities and should not consist of family members or close friends of management.

- The types of services offered—there should be a wide variety of services offered such as budget counseling; debt counseling; and housing counseling for those who want to rent or buy a house, are delinquent on their mortgage loans, or are facing foreclosure. The agency should be authorized by the Executive Office of U.S. Trustees (EOUST) to provide both the pre-filing credit counseling and the pre-discharge personal financial management education required by the Bankruptcy Abuse Prevention and Consumer Protection Act of 2005.

- While authorization by the EOUST to provide these services is not an endorsement of the agency, it is a confirmation that the credit counseling agency has been rigorously reviewed and found to be acceptable. By offering a wide variety of services, the agency demonstrates its commitment to individualized solutions to individual problems rather than forcing everyone into a "one-size-fits-all" debt management program.

- Reasonable fees or contributions—in the past, 501(c)3 credit counseling agencies were able to offer their services at extremely low cost or at no cost due to the generous support of creditors and grant funders. Over the past decade, the financial support received from creditors has fallen to abysmally low levels, forcing credit counseling agencies to charge fees for services that once were free, and to assess higher fees for services that were once available at minimal charge. Still, the agency should make every effort to keep fees as low as possible without endangering the ability of the agency to provide much needed help; and it should be willing to waive fees when collecting them would impose undue financial hardship on the client.

- How counseling is provided—can you meet with the counselor in person, or is counseling provided only by telephone or only through the Internet? A good agency will make every possible effort to accommodate your preferences.

- An agency willing to work with all of your creditors—the agency should not "cherry pick" only those creditors that will provide the agency with generous financial support. A reputable agency will review your entire financial situation and provide the help that is in the client's best interests, not in their own best interests.

- Enrollment in a debt management program that provides for your first payment to be disbursed to your creditors—some agencies keep that first payment and pay their own operating expenses with the money. If a client was not past due before entering into one of these first-payment plans, the plan will put them into a "past due" status by not sending that first payment to the creditors.

- Willingness to give you more than just fifteen or twenty minutes of their time—look for an agency that devotes a full hour or longer to understanding *your* situation and looking for appropriate solutions to the problems that you are facing.

- Compliance with your state's licensing laws—while some states have no licensing requirements, others have very strict laws and arduous licensing requirements. If an agency can't be counted on to obey the laws of the state in which it is doing business, do you really want to trust it to do "the right thing" with your money?

- Client funds that are placed into a separate trust account and are not co-mingled with the agency's operating funds—this provides the greatest possible assurance that your funds will go to your creditors.

## Rebuild Credit

A credit report and the resulting credit score is nothing but a report on behavioral patterns. The best way for a person to rebuild credit is to demonstrate new behavior patterns.

If your credit report shows that you are paying certain debts on time and as agreed, continue to do this. Remember, the longer the history of on-time payments the better.

Establish new accounts and demonstrate a pattern of borrowing money and repaying it on time and as agreed. One client I met with rebuilt his credit this way:

> Paul received a small inheritance of $2,000 when his aunt died. To prevent himself from frivolously spending this money, he had placed it in a certificate of deposit at his local credit union. He knew that, to rebuild his credit, he needed to demonstrate a pattern of borrowing and repaying as agreed.

> Paul went to the credit union and negotiated a small ($500) short-term loan that was to be repaid over a six-month period. Because a loan that is secured by collateral is charged a lower interest rate, he pledged the certificate of deposit as collateral for the loan. The credit union told him that he could get a still lower interest rate if he

*authorized the credit union to automatically deduct pay-*
*ments from his checking or savings account every month*
*until the loan was repaid.*

*Paul deposited the $500 that he had borrowed into his*
*savings account and authorized the credit union to auto-*
*matically deduct the loan payment from that account. In*
*essence, he was repaying the debt with the same money*
*he had borrowed, plus the much smaller amount of inter-*
*est on the loan.*

At the end of the six months, the loan was repaid in full and Paul had a new entry on his credit report that demonstrated that he had repaid the loan as agreed. Yes, it did cost him a little bit of interest, but we can only guess how much interest this transaction may have saved him on future loans because he had raised his credit score.

## Factors That Cannot Be Used When Calculating a Credit Score

When talking about the factors that cannot be used in calculating a person's credit score, let's begin by citing "all the usual suspects": race, creed, color, age (unless the applicant is too young to sign a contract), national origin, gender, and marital status. These factors spring to mind because they are so well known and have a history in our national consciousness. In addition, the Equal Credit Opportunity Act (ECOA) prohibits the use of the following additional factors:

**Receipt of Public Assistance**—income is income, regardless of the source. If the applicant's total income is sufficient to service the debt, the source of that income is irrelevant. This includes alimony, child support, and separate maintenance payments. However, the creditor can ask for proof that income from these sources is consistently paid on time.

**Where the Applicant Lives**—in the past, "redlining" was often used to indicate certain neighborhoods where money could not or would not be loaned, primarily due to the racial composition of the neighborhood. ECOA and several other federal laws now outlaw this practice.

**Interest Rates on Existing Accounts**—the interest rate you are charged on your older accounts was determined by your earlier credit history and credit score. Likewise, the history and score will determine the annual percentage rate on a new account. However, the interest rates on those other accounts are not a factor.

**Soft Inquiries**—to fully appreciate this last point, it's important to know the difference between a hard inquiry and a soft inquiry.

- Hard inquiries occur when you ask a lender to loan you money. Before making that decision, the lender will obtain a copy of your credit report, review the history and score, and make a decision.

- Soft inquiries occur without your knowledge. For example, the Acme Credit Card is trying to decide if it wants to send you one of those infamous "Congratulations, you're pre-approved!" letters. It looks at your credit report to decide if you are likely to meet its loan underwriting standards. You did not ask Acme to do this; it did it entirely on its own.

While the hard inquiry impacts your credit score, the soft inquiry does not.

## How to Get Your Credit Report

As we noted in Chapter 12, it is *always* a good idea to obtain a current copy of your credit report and review it on a regular basis. Check it for accuracy and guard against identity theft.

You can obtain a copy of your credit report from each of the three major credit reporting bureaus—Equifax, Experian, and TransUnion—by contacting them directly. They will charge you for the report, and it may or may not include a credit score (either a FICO score or a Vantage score). Here again is their contact information:

| Equifax | Experian | TransUnion |
|---|---|---|
| P.O. Box 740241 | P.O. Box 2002 | P.O. Box 1000 |
| Atlanta, GA 30374 | Allen, TX 75013 | Chester, PA 19022 |
| 800-685-1111 | 888-397-3742 | 800-888-4213 |
| www.equifax.com | www.experian.com | www.transunion.com |

Another way to get a copy of your report is to visit the website www.annualcreditreport.com. This site was created as a result of the passage of the Fair and Accurate Credit Transactions Act of 2003, which ensures that each consumer can receive a copy of his or her report from each reporting bureau once each year at no cost. The report is free, but if you want a score, you will have to pay for it.

## How to Read a Credit Report

The parts of a mock credit report are shown below. Let's look at the report in two sections and by column headers.

This first section of the report provides the scores (in the Product Score column) and the primary factors that created this score. In the report below, we can see that all three bureaus indicate that the most significant factor in the score is the presence of serious delinquencies. In addition, the bureaus consider both whether accounts have been sent to collections and whether there is an appearance in public records, such as a legal judgment that has been obtained to enforce the collection of a debt.

| Data Sources | | |
|---|---|---|
| Product Score | Factor Information | Data Source |
| FICO Classic<br><br>527 | 038 – Serious delinquency and public record or collection filed<br><br>013 – Time since delinquency is too recent or unknown<br><br>010 – Proportion of balances to credit limits is too high on bank revolving or other revolving accounts<br><br>020 – Length of time since derogatory public record or collection is too short | TUC |
| Beacon<br><br>578 | 038 – Serious delinquency and public record or collection filed<br><br>013 – Time since delinquency is too recent or unknown<br><br>010 – Proportion of balances to credit limits is too high on bank revolving or other revolving accounts<br><br>020 – Length of time since derogatory public record or collection is too short | EFX |
| FICO Classic 04<br><br>519 | 038 – Serious delinquency and public record or collection filed<br><br>010 – Proportion of balances to credit limits is too high on bank revolving or other revolving accounts<br><br>013 – Time since delinquency is too recent or un-known<br><br>020 – Length of time since derogatory public record or collection is too short | EXP |

FIGURE 13.1

| Credit History | | | | | | | | | | | |
|---|---|---|---|---|---|---|---|---|---|---|---|
| Credit Grantor | Date Reported | Credit Highest | Bal-ance | Monthly Payment Amount | Accoun Type | Months Reviewed | Times 30 Days Past Due | Times 60 Days Past Due | Times 90 Days Past Due | Data Source | |
| Account Number | Date Opened | Credit Limit | | | Status | | | | | | |
| Acme 1234 5678 | 1 – 11 9 – 05 | 11092 9500 | 10555 | 385 | R-5 | 64 | 01 | 01 | 06 | TUC | |
| C&P Collections X579 Original Creditor - Fly By Night Credit | 1 – 11 12 - 10 | 4000 | 5432 | 5432 | Del 120 I-9 | 1 | 00 | 00 | 00 | XPN | |
| MY Home Ln 86423579 Real Estate | 1 – 11 4 - 01 | 150000 124951 | 124951 | 963 | M-1 Pd as Agreed | 117 | 00 | 00 | 00 | EFX XPN TUC | |

FIGURE 13.2

In the entries above, we can see the following information:

**Credit Grantor/Account Number**—our consumer has three open creditors: the Acme Department Store, C&P Collections, and the My Home Loan Mortgage Company. To help prevent identity theft, the credit bureaus often provide only partial account numbers so that a thief cannot use the account as a reference.

**Date Reported/Date Opened**—using the Acme account as an example, we see that Acme's most recent report was made to the credit bureau in January 2011. We also see that the account was opened in September 2005. Furthermore, C&P Collections made a report in January 2011, but it didn't become the creditor/collector of record until December 2010.

**Credit Highest/Credit Limit**—either when the Acme account was opened or at some time after it was opened, the credit limit was set at $9,500. The highest balance carried on the account, however, got up to $11,092. On a more positive note, we can see that our consumer borrowed $150,000 from My Home Loan Mortgage Company to buy the house, and the outstanding balance is now down to $124,951.

**Monthly Payment Amount**—the Monthly Payment Amount shows the minimum the consumer should be paying on the account each month. Thus, we can determine that the monthly mortgage payment is $963 (principle and interest only).

**Account Type/Status**—each line of credit is assigned an alpha-numeric grade which indicates the type of loan that was made and whether it is paid up to date or not. "R" indicates that this is a revolving charge account. "I" indicates an installment loan. "M" indicates a mortgage loan. The numeric character "1" means that the account is paid current, "2" means it is 30 days past due, "3" means it is 60 days past due, "4" means it is 90 days past due, "5" means it is 120 days past due, and so on. A "9" indicates that the account has been sent to collections.

**Months Reviewed**—the number of months of credit history that was reviewed for each account is important information. The loan from My Home Loan Mortgage Company, for example, was reviewed for its activity over the past 117 months. The longer the review period, the more context that is provided to the creditor looking at the report to decide if credit should be granted. For example, one account was reviewed for only a two-month period and shows 30 days past due one time. Meanwhile, another account on the report was reviewed for the past 48 months and shows 30 days past due one time. A prospective lender will naturally feel more confident looking at the 48-month record.

**Times X Days Past Due**—the three "Times" columns tell us how many times the account has been 30, 60, and 90 days past due.

**Data Source**—the Data Source column tells us which bureau made the report. It is possible that the debt was reported to only one bureau (as is the case for both Acme and C&P); or it may have been reported to more than one bureau (such as My Home Loan Mortgage Company which was reported to all three bureaus).

## What to Do If the Report Is Inaccurate

It is not at all uncommon for credit reports to contain errors. Every year thousands of errors are found in credit reports. Fortunately, the Fair Credit Reporting Act (FCRA) guarantees citizens certain rights when the reports are wrong.

To correct an error, start by filing a dispute with the credit reporting bureau. Some people attempt to do this by telephone. However, verbal disputes, in my opinion, aren't worth the paper that they were never written on. Send a letter to the bureau whose report contains the inaccurate information. Explain the inaccuracy and request that the report be corrected. Here is a sample letter:

*Dear Sir or Madam:*

*I dispute the following accounts and request that they be corrected in my credit file. Under the Fair Credit Reporting Act (FCRA), I request that these items be investigated and/or deleted from my credit record.*

- *Ninth National Bank #9753-8642-7419—this is not my account. Please remove it from my report.*

- *Clawback and Pillager Collections #666—this account was paid in full to original creditor, Bank of the Big River. Please remove this account from my report.*

*I assume that 30 days constitutes reasonable time for verification of these entries, unless you immediately notify me otherwise. It should be understood that failure to verify these items within 30 days constitutes reason to promptly drop the information from my file according to the Fair Credit Reporting Act.*

*For the purpose of identification, I have enclosed a copy of my driver's license, Social Security card, and a current utility bill that confirms my mailing address.*

*Please notify me when these items have been deleted. You may send a copy of my credit report to the address listed below. According to the Fair Credit Reporting Act, there should be no charge for this service.*

*Sincerely,*

_____

*Sam **O**. Samples*
*123 Jump Street*

*Orlando, FL 328xx*

*xxx-xx-xxxx*
*Social Security Number*

Under the terms of the Fair Credit Reporting Act, the credit bureau must investigate this dispute and respond to the consumer within a reasonable period of time. Based on the timeframe contained in the letter, 30 days is considered to be reasonable. It is always a good idea to send the dispute letter "Certified/Return Receipt Requested" so that you know when the letter was received; the date from which the reasonable period of time is measured.

When the response is received, it will most likely fall into one of these three categories:

- Category #1—we have investigated your dispute of the Ninth National Bank account #9753-8642-7419-xxxx and found that it is accurately reported. For additional information, please contact Ninth National Bank, 3579 Broken Limb Street, Two Bumps on a Log, South Dakota.

- Category #2—we have investigated your dispute of the Clawback and Pillager Collections account #666 and found that this debt was paid in full to the original creditor, and your credit report has been corrected.

- Category #3—we have investigated your dispute of the Clawback and Pillager Collections account #666 and have been unable to verify information regarding this account. It has been removed from your report.

If the credit reporting bureau fails to respond within a reasonable time, send a follow-up letter to the credit bureau that has failed to respond. Such a letter could be worded as follows:

*Dear Sir or Madam:*

*On [insert date], I wrote to you disputing the following report entries and requesting that incorrect information be either corrected or deleted.*

- *Ninth National Bank #9753-8642-7419—this is not my account. Please remove it from my report.*

- *Clawback and Pillager Collections #666—this account was paid in full to original creditor, Bank of the Big River. Please remove this account from my report.*

*Under the Fair Credit Reporting Act (FCRA), you had thirty (30) days to investigate these items and either affirm their validity or delete them from my credit record. It is understood that failure to verify these items within 30 days constitutes reason to promptly drop the information from my file according to Section 623(a)(1)(B) and 623(a)(3) of the FCRA. Inasmuch as you have not responded to my request of [insert date], I must now respectfully request that the disputed entries be deleted from my credit report.*

*Please notify me when these items have been deleted. You may send a copy of my credit report to the address below. According to the Fair Credit Reporting Act, there should be no charge for this service.*

---

*Sam **O**. Samples*
*123 Jump Street*

*Orlando, FL 328xx*

*xxx-xx-xxxx*
*Social Security Number*

## Conclusion

Clearly, credit reports affect all aspects of life.

- The cost of borrowing money is impacted as low scores raise interest rates and the cost of borrowing money

- Unfavorable credit histories can thwart job searches by even the most qualified candidates

- Poor bill paying habits can even increase the cost of insurance

Credit reporting bureaus typically use two different scoring methodologies

- FICO models are based on five scoring factors that yield scores between 300 and 850

- Vantage models are based on six scoring factors resulting in scores that range between 501 and 990

- Each lender determines the acceptable score at which a borrower qualifies for a loan

Favorable credit histories can be established, and unfavorable histories rebuilt, by

- Paying bills on time

- Keeping outstanding balances below 50 percent of credit limits

- Ensuring that accounts show sufficient recent activity to avoid closure for inactivity

- Resolving old debts and demonstrating a behavioral pattern of borrowing and repaying debts on time as agreed

- Having a good balance between the amount of credit currently in use and the total available credit

Unfortunately, credit reports cannot be established or rebuilt overnight. Both take time to demonstrate that new and consistent patterns of borrowing and repaying have been firmly established.

If you find yourself overwhelmed by debts, you have options. You can

- Pay the debts in full

- Attempt to settle the debts for less than the full balance

- Contact a non-profit credit counseling agency and obtain assistance in creating a repayment program in which the creditors make concessions that will help you repay the debts, in full, over time

When contacting a credit counseling agency, there is a number of factors that you should look for to ensure that you are working with an agency that is truly working on your behalf rather than for their own benefit.

There are three major credit reporting bureaus (Equifax, Experian, and TransUnion) that you want to have accurate credit information about you. Under the Fair Credit Reporting Act you can get a copy of your credit report annually from each one at no charge, and you should know how to read these credit reports. If there is an inaccuracy, you have rights to correct them.

It is the responsibility of each and every one of us to check our own report and make certain that the report is accurate and speaks highly of us.

## CHAPTER 14

# Home Ownership

*So You Think You're Ready to Be a Homeowner!*

"A house is made of walls and beams; a home is built with love and dreams."
— Author Unknown

It's the American Dream—a little house in the suburbs with a white picket fence. In theory, it's what everyone is supposed to aspire to; and, for many, it is the dream. For others, however, it is not the best choice. The first step in determining if you are ready to become a homeowner is to weigh the advantages and disadvantages of both renting (or leasing) and buying to determine what is best for you.

## Renting (or Leasing) vs. Owning

### Advantages of Renting

Are you new in town and not sure where you want to live? A smart strategy is to rent a house or apartment and live in the area you think you might be interested in. After living in the neighborhood for a while, you will be in a better position to decide if that's the area where you want to put down roots. If you decide that it's not your idea of home, no problem—move and try another neighborhood. This is perhaps one of the biggest advantages of renting—you are not "tied" to one place.

Do you cringe when something breaks down and doesn't work? As a renter, you do not need to worry about it; just call the manager and ask that maintenance come and fix it. Best of all, you don't have to pay for the repairs. It is just another advantage of renting.

Finally, somebody other than you gets the annual bill for property taxes.

**Disadvantages of Renting**

Perhaps the biggest disadvantage of renting is what you don't have to show for all the rent you pay. A stack of rent receipts has never built anyone's net worth; except for the landlord's.

In addition, if you don't like something about the place you are renting, say the color of the carpet, you can't change it. Nor can you change the color of the paint on the walls or anything else about the house without the landlord's permission.

**Advantages of Owning**

For many, the first and biggest advantage is the tax deductibility of the interest paid on a mortgage loan. This is, for many people, a significant thing. It has the potential to substantially lower taxable income.

Another big advantage of ownership is the fact that, over time, the owner builds equity. Simply stated, equity is the profit that will be left if the house is sold and the mortgage paid off. If the value of the house goes up from the price it was purchased at, the equity builds even faster. When the mortgage loan has been fully repaid, the house is yours; free and clear!

One other advantage should be noted here. If you want to make a change, paint a room another color or remodel the kitchen, you are free to do so. No one's permission is required.

## Disadvantages of Owning

First, you may need to have enough money for a down payment. While home mortgage loans have customarily required a down payment equal to 10 percent of the purchase price, there are financing programs available that allow a person to buy a house with a smaller down payment. In fact, there are currently two mortgage programs that allow 100% financing. Additionally, there are often down payment assistance programs that can help first-time homebuyers with this. If the buyer cannot put down 20 percent of the purchase price, the lender will require that the buyer pay for private mortgage insurance (PMI) to protect the lender against default. The private mortgage insurance companies have developed a program in which the entire premium for the PMI is paid at the time of closing so that no monthly premium payments are required.

Another disadvantage of ownership is the amount of money that must be available to close the purchase. The buyer must have sufficient cash to pay his or her share of the closing costs, which vary from state to state but could be as much as 5% of the purchase price.

A third big disadvantage of owning your own home is that, when something breaks or needs maintenance, you, the owner, must either fix it or pay someone else to fix it for you. No one does these things for you without additional cost.

Another consideration is what to do if you want or need to move. Before you can move, you may first have to sell the house and pay off the existing mortgage. If the house has appreciated in value and can be sold for more than is owed, as the owner, you pocket the profit and use it as a down payment on your next home. Conversely, if the house has depreciated and cannot be sold for the amount that is owed, there are two options:

- Bring enough money to the closing table to pay off the difference between the selling price and the amount that is owed

- Convince the lender to approve a short sale, wherein the lender agrees to accept less than the amount that is owed as payment in full

## What Kind of House Do You Want to Own?

Once you have decided that owning a home is better for you than renting, the next decision is what kind of house you want to own. Just as there are many different kinds of home buyers, there are different kinds of homes. Here are a few of the options:

- Single Family Home—this is a free-standing house on its own lot. Typically, it has its own front and back yard and it is not connected to any other residence.

- Condominium—condominiums are individually owned homes attached to one another under a common roof. Frequently condominium developments also have shared facilities that can be used by all residents; for example, recreation and fitness centers, pools, parks, and playgrounds. They also have a condominium owners' association that creates and enforces the by-laws and covenants (rules and regulations) that govern the building(s) in the development. The association is also responsible for maintenance and improvements to the facilities. Recently condominium developments of detached housing units have been created. As always, if you consider purchasing one of these units, read the association documents carefully.

- Townhouse—while condo developments tend to spread out over an area of ground (horizontal development), townhomes tend to be vertical developments; that is, they are usually multi-floor units. They combine the privacy of a single family home with the common exterior maintenance of a condominium.

- Duplexes—a duplex looks much like a single family home in that it is a free-standing building separate from other buildings. However, it is actually two separate residences under one roof. They may have separate yards, or they may share a common front and back yard. The owner has the option of renting both units or living in one unit and renting the other in order to reduce the net cost.

## New Construction or Existing House

As a home buyer, you have the choice of buying an existing house or buying a house that has previously been lived in. There are advantages to both.

- New Construction—one advantage of buying a brand new house is the opportunity to decorate and landscape according to your own preferences. If the landscaping has not been installed yet, you may be able to choose the type of lawn, flowering plants, bushes, and trees that you want planted. Remember, though, that the landscaping may need time to mature before it looks like you envision it. An alternative is that the purchase of a house under construction often provides allowances for not only the landscaping but also the interior amenities like carpet, tile, and hardwood flooring. New construction offers the opportunity to customize the house to some degree. On the downside, a new home may be more expensive than a pre-existing house, and may not be ready for occupancy when you want to move into it.

- Pre-Existing House—Depending on how motivated the seller is, you may have more bargaining power when negotiating the price of a pre-existing house. The house will likely include appliances and fixtures. In many cases, it is ready for occupancy as soon as the sale is closed. On the other hand, if the house is a "fixer-upper," it may require extensive repairs, maintenance, or modernization before you can move in. Repairs can become very costly if there are problems with heating and air conditioning systems, a cracked foundation, or a roof that needs to be replaced. It is always a sound practice to have a thorough inspection performed by a licensed home inspector who can identify problems or potential problems that could affect the price of the house and/or your ability to live in it.

## Are You Ready to Buy?

Now that you have decided that you want to buy and you know the kind of house that you want to buy, the next step is to decide if you are ready to buy now. Here is a series of questions that you should answer. Some address your ability to obtain a mortgage loan; others address your ability to maintain the house and make monthly payments after buying it.

- Do you have money for the down payment, or are you eligible for a down payment assistance program? Do you have the bank statements that verify assets and savings ?

- Do you have the cash to pay closing costs?

- Do you have a stable income?

- Have you had steady employment for at least the past two to three years? Do you have the documentation that your lender will require including W-2 Forms and recent tax returns that prove your income and confirmation of employment from your employer?

- Can you afford the monthly mortgage payments plus the property taxes, maintenance expenses, and repairs that may be needed now and in the future?

- Do you have a good credit history; and, is your credit report accurate so that you can qualify for the most favorable loan terms?

- Can you obtain pre-approval or pre-qualify for a mortgage loan?

  o Pre-Approval is an informal process that will confirm that you can qualify for a loan and how much money you may be eligible to borrow. However, it does not guarantee that you will get the loan and you are under no obligation to borrow. The pre-approval is valid for a limited amount of time.

  o Pre-Qualification is a formal procedure in which a loan is approved up to a specific maximum amount. When you are pre-qualified, you can assure the seller that your loan is ready to go to the closing table and complete the sale.

## Different Types of Mortgage Loans

Since we know that there are different kinds of homes and home buyers, it only makes sense that there are different types of mortgage loans. Here are a few of the more common types.

- **Conventional Loans**—these bank loans are not backed by the Federal Housing Administration (FHA). A minimum down payment of 5 percent is required; however, it could be as high as 20 percent depending on the geographic area in which the house is located. If equity in the house is less than 22 percent of its current value, private mortgage insurance will be required. To qualify for this loan, the buyer's monthly mortgage payment (principle and interest only) cannot exceed 32 percent of his or her gross monthly income; and the combined payments on the mortgage loan, credit cards, car loans, and any other debts cannot be greater than 43 percent of the gross monthly income. The bank statements that will be required as part of the paperwork to qualify for the loan must demonstrate that the buyer has a minimum of two monthly payments in reserve. Interest rates on these loans can either be fixed for the duration of the loan, or they can vary, rising and falling based on a specified index.

- **FHA Loans**—these loans are guaranteed by the Federal Housing Administration. They require a minimum 3.5 percent down payment, and money received in the form of gifts, loans, or grants from acceptable sources can be used to make the down payment and pay closing costs. Again, because the equity in the house is lower than 20 percent of current value, private mortgage insurance will be required to protect the lender against default. When the buyer uses FHA financing, the monthly mortgage payment cannot exceed 32 percent of the buyer's gross monthly income, and the monthly payments on all debts combined cannot be greater than 43 percent of the gross monthly income. As with conventional loans, the interest rates can be fixed or variable. Unlike conventional loans, there is no requirement to have monthly payments in reserve. The buyer does need sufficient cash to pay his or her share of the closing costs, which vary from state to state. Finally, there is a limit on the maximum loan amount, which is determined by FHA guidelines.

- **The Department of Veterans Affairs Loans**—these loans are available to veterans and widows/widowers of veterans. They are guaranteed by the Department of Veterans Affairs. VA Loans do not require down payments and they do not require Private Mortgage Insurance. Instead, the borrower pays a VA funding fee. The funding fee is paid at the time of closing and can be paid in full by the veteran or the seller, or can be financed as part of the mortgage loan. It should be noted that this funding fee is waived for disabled veterans. These loans offer only fixed interest rates, and they do not use debt ratios as a qualification standard. Like FHA loans, there is a maximum loan amount, and gifts, loans, or grants from acceptable sources can be used to pay closing costs. VA Loans are available only to veterans who have met specific requirements with regard to their military service. To determine if you are eligible, contact the Veterans Administration or visit this website:

www. http://benefits.va.gov/homeloans/

- **USDA or Rural Housing Loans**—these loans are available only in areas where the government says the population is under 10,000 people. The program is also limited to individuals who meet certain income limits. A loan guarantee fee, which can be included in the amount to be financed, must be paid at the time of closing and the buyer also pays for Private Mortgage Insurance.

- **Balloon Mortgages**—balloon mortgages typically carry lower initial interest rates so that the borrower may qualify for a higher loan amount. The interest rates are fixed for a specific number of years, often 3, 5, or 7 years. When the initial period ends, the balance becomes due in full, or the mortgage can be refinanced at current market interest rates. When the loan is refinanced, the monthly payment could be higher or lower depending on the new interest rate. While this type of mortgage used to be fairly commonplace, they are nearly impossible to find as of this writing due to government restrictions.

- **Construction and Construction-to-Permanent Loans**—when a person chooses to buy land and build a house on it, he or she may obtain a construction mortgage loan. The loan will pay for the land and the materials and labor to construct the house. When the building is completed, the loan must be converted to a regular mortgage loan. Alternatively, the buyer can obtain a construction-to-permanent loan which automatically converts from a construction loan to a regular mortgage loan so that the buyer needs to pay closing costs only one time.

## Ability To Repay (ATR) Rule and Qualifying Mortgages

With the implementation of provisions of the Dodd-Frank Mortgage Reform Act beginning in January 2014, three new rules regarding home mortgage loans significantly impact how a borrower is reviewed as the loan is being underwritten.

- **The Ability To Repay Rule**—applies to all residential mortgages. Under this rule, the lender must make a good faith effort to determine two factors: (1) that the borrower does, in fact, have the ability to repay the loan and (2) how much money the borrower has left each month after satisfying of his or her debts. To make these determinations, the lender must consider the following factors:

    o   The borrower's current income or assets

    o   The borrower's current employment status including seasonal employment

    o   The borrower's credit history

    o   The monthly payment for the mortgage

    o   The monthly payments for other mortgage loans that the borrower obtains at the same time

    o   The monthly payment for other mortgage-related expenses such as property taxes

    o   Other outstanding debts that the borrower owes

    o   The borrower's Debt-To-Income (DTI) ratio

- **The Qualified Mortgage (QM) Rule**—is a subset of the Ability To Repay Rule and requires that the lender adhere to specific standards in order to qualify the loan for resale on the secondary mortgage market. If the lender is to be able to sell the loan to a third party such as Federal National Mortgage Association (FNMA) or Government National Mortgage Association (GNMA), the loan must have

o Specific loan features that must either be included or excluded in the mortgage document

o A limit on the points and fees imposed on the borrower

o Met required underwriting features when determining if the loan is to be approved

Additionally, the QM Rule creates two categories of legal liability for compliant loans.

o Safe Harbor—provides the lender with a higher level of protection against litigation. When the loan falls into this category, the loan is conclusively presumed to comply with the Ability To Repay requirements.

o Rebuttable Presumption—When the loan is in this category, the borrower can argue that the creditor violated the ATR requirements by showing that, at the time the loan was made, the borrower did not have enough income left to meet living expenses after making the mortgage payment and payments on other debts.

- **The Qualified Residential Mortgage Rule**—is designed to eliminate riskier loans. When the loan is a Qualified Mortgage, the lender will be able to sell the entire loan to a buyer on the secondary mortgage market. But, when the loan does not meet the QM requirements, the lender will be required to retain a portion of the loan on its books. In other words, because the lender cannot sell the entire loan, it will suffer a loss if the borrower defaults.

It's important to understand the impact of these rules on the loan process. Because the lender must now verify all of the borrower's income and assets with third party records and must be able to show the borrower's ability to repay the loan in order to make the loan a Qualified Residential Mortgage, the borrower is going to feel as though he or she is be scrutinized under a powerful microscope. For example, if the borrower's bank records show that there has been a deposit of more than $50 that did not come from the borrower's verifiable employment income, the PATRIOT ACT requires that the borrower must now provide written proof of where the money came from in order to demonstrate that the money is not part of a money laundering scheme.

## The Components of a Mortgage Payment

When you make your mortgage payment each month, you are actually making a payment that covers several obligations. Often referred to as "PITI," the components have nothing to do with either sympathy or empathy.

- **P—the principle repayment.** This is the amount of the payment that pays back part of the loan itself and reduces the outstanding balance. In the beginning years of the loan, only a minimal part of each monthly payment is applied to the repayment of the loan, and the balance is reduced by a very small amount.

- **I—the interest payment.** Simply stated, interest is the fee paid for using someone else's money. Home loan repayment plans are very heavily weighted toward the payment of interest in the early years and this is the reason that nearly all of each monthly payment is comprised of interest.

- **T—a portion of the annual property tax assessment.** When 1/12 of the property taxes is paid as part of each monthly mortgage payment, this amount of money is placed into an escrow account. This account is, in essence, a savings account maintained by the lender or the title company where funds are accumulated with which to pay the tax assessment when the annual bill is due. It is not required that the property owner include

234

the property tax payments in the monthly loan payment. However, it can be a good idea if the owner does not want to worry about where to find the money when the assessment is due. While this might appear to contradict my earlier admonition about not letting someone else earn interest on your money, the peace of mind might well be worth the foregone interest.

- **I—a monthly installment toward the payment of insurance premiums due each year.** Like the escrowing of funds for the payment of the property taxes above, 1/12th of the annual cost of homeowners insurance, flood insurance, and private mortgage insurance can be paid as a part of each monthly mortgage payment and placed into the escrow account so that funds are available to pay the annual bill each year. Again, this is not required, but is strongly encouraged for the same reason as cited above.

## Private Mortgage Insurance

Private mortgage insurance has been mentioned several times above. Lenders have known for years that the more personal money a home buyer has invested in the purchase of a home, the less likely the individual is to default on the loan. The buyer simply has too much personal money at stake and will do whatever is necessary to ensure that the mortgage payment is made every month. For this reason, it used to be required that the buyer had to have enough cash to make a large down payment, the amount of which may have varied over time.

The problem, of course, is that it is very difficult for a buyer to accumulate sufficient funds for these large payments; some would say impossible. Consider that the census bureau reports that the median price of a new home sold in the United States in January 2010 was $218,200. A 10 percent down payment would require $21,820; a 20 percent down payment would require $43,640.

To make it easier for individuals and families to own their own homes, different mortgage loan programs have made it possible for buyers to purchase their homes with as little as 3.5 percent of the purchase price as a down payment; veterans need no down payment with a VA loan.

To protect themselves from the higher risk of default that comes with low down payments, lenders require that an insurance policy be purchased that will reimburse the lender if the borrower defaults on the loan. This program is known as private mortgage insurance (PMI). The cost of the PMI can be paid with a single payment when the loan closes; or, the buyer can make monthly payments as part of their mortgage payment.

When a home owner has a conventional loan and the owner's equity in the house rises to 22 percent or more of the home's fair market value, the owner can cancel the PMI. In the case of FHA loans, the monthly premium for PMI is paid for the life of the loan.

## Mortgage Fraud

When it comes to mortgage fraud, deception comes in several flavors. Here is a look at the most prevalent forms.

- **Fraud for Property**—a significant portion of the housing bubble was created when potential buyers were willing to do whatever was necessary to qualify for the purchase of a house before prices went even higher. An unethical lender, knowing that the potential buyer might not have the financial resources to qualify for the loan, tells the buyer that there is a way to make the buyer "look" qualified.

    o  One way to do this is to falsify documents so that it appears that the buyer has more financial resources than are actually available.

    o  Another way is to use a "no-document loan" or a "stated income loan." This type of loan requires no documentation or proof of income; just that the buyer says, "Yes, that's how much I make."

In either case, the borrower receives a loan that he or she is not qualified for and is likely to default on the first time something goes wrong. By that time the unethical lender has collected and spent a commission that should not have been paid, and the house can be foreclosed on and sold again.

- **Fraud for Profit**—in this type of fraud, a lender creates a false credit profile for a potential borrower so that it appears the borrower is more creditworthy than he or she really is. Or, in order for the buyer to obtain a loan for which the property does not qualify, an appraiser is paid to inflate the value of the property so that it appears to be worth more than its fair market value.

- **Foreclosure Fraud**—as home loan default has increased in recent years, so has the number of fraud cases involving methods of stopping or preventing foreclosures. A homeowner struggling to make the monthly payment who does not want to lose the house is an easy mark for this type of fraud. Out of nowhere, a kindly individual appears and says, "Don't worry, we can save your home and make this all go away!" The homeowner, grasping at straws, is relieved and gladly follows the guidance of the fraudster.

  o Perhaps the homeowner is asked to pay fees for work that will be done at some unspecified time by the fraudster and his or her company. The fees are paid in advance and the only thing that goes away is the homeowner's money.

  o On the other hand, the homeowner is asked to sign the deed over to the fraudster with the assurance that the mortgage company "can't take the house away from you if it's not in your name." Having transferred title to the house, the homeowner suddenly finds himself or herself on the receiving end of an eviction notice and is informed that the house has been sold and the new owners are ready to move in. Meanwhile, the mortgage company has received no money and is pursuing foreclosure; the individual who has purchased the house has no clear title and does not own the house and has lost whatever money was paid to the fraudster; and the original owner who paid the fraudster for all this help is still on the hook for the balance of the mortgage and will lose whatever equity may have accrued in the property when the lender takes possession.

If you or someone you know wants to be sure you are financially ready to buy a house, it's a good idea to seek pre-purchase housing counseling from a reputable housing counselor. Likewise, if you or someone you know is struggling to retain possession of a home, a reputable housing counselor who is experienced in mortgage delinquency or foreclosure prevention counseling may be able to identify strategies that will enable the owner to retain the house.

When looking for a reputable housing counselor, look for an agency that has received approval from the Department of Housing and Urban Development (HUD) to provide housing counseling services. Alternatively, the National Foundation for Credit Counseling (NFCC) has many member agencies that are authorized to provide housing counseling services.

## Selecting a Real Estate Agent

When it comes to buying or selling a house, everybody likes to feel like an expert. Anyone can hang out his or her shingle and claim to be the agent you want representing your best interests in the transaction. To decide on the person you want handling the negotiations and details for you, what should you look for? Here is a partial list of traits you may want to consider.

- What is your agent's role?

    o First and foremost, your agent should represent you and should help you obtain the best deal that can be negotiated. Your agent is your guide through the entire process and should help you navigate the process with the least difficulty.

    o A good agent will help you determine the price range of the homes you should be viewing and help you look only at houses within that range.

    o Your agent should help negotiate the purchase price and represent your interests by structuring the deal in a way that saves you money.

    o The agent should be able to answer questions before and at the closing.

- Whom does the agent represent?

    o Unless you specifically retain a "buyer's broker," the agent represents the seller. You may want to retain the services of a buyer's broker to ensure that the agent is representing you. If you decide to hire this individual, be sure to ask who pays his or her fee and how that fee is determined.

- Where can I find an agent?

    o Ask business associates, family members, and friends for the names of agents that they have worked with and can recommend.

    o Attend open houses and talk with the agents who are showing the houses.

- Does the agent belong to a professional association and sub-scribe to a code of ethics?

  - o The National Association of Realtors® is undoubtedly the best known and respected association of real estate agents. By joining this association, Realtors pledge that they will conduct themselves in accordance with the As-sociation's Code of Ethics.

## You've Found Your Dream House—Now What?

OK, you finally found it—the house you've been dreaming of. What do you do now?

- **Determine a fair price**—rarely is the price the seller is asking the actual selling price. Compare the asking price to the prices paid for similar homes in the area, the "comps." The lender will obtain an appraisal, and the comps are one of the factors that the appraiser will look at.

- **Select a lender and review the terms of the loan**—the lender is required to provide you with a Good Faith Estimate that shows the following information:

  - o The loan amount

  - o The interest rate on the loan and whether it can increase after closing

  - o The monthly principal and interest payment

  - o If the loan has a prepayment penalty, the maximum it can be, and for how many years the loan is subject to a prepayment penalty

  - o If there is a balloon payment due

- o The monthly cost, if any, of Private Mortgage Insurance

- o The monthly deposit into the escrow account to cover taxes and homeowners insurance

- o The estimated total monthly payment (PITI)

- o Estimated closing costs and the amount of money that must be brought to the closing table

- **Hire a licensed home inspector**—the inspector's job is to look for any current and/or potential problems with the house. The inspector will examine

  - o The exterior of the structure including the roof, chimney, porch, and deck to ensure that all are free of defect

  - o The foundation, walls, and floors to determine if there are any cracks that would indicate a serious structural problem

  - o The plumbing to determine if there is sufficient water pressure, any leaks, and if waste lines are properly vented

  - o The adequacy of the electrical system for the house's needs; tests of all electrical outlets, the wiring, and the circuit breakers and fuses

  - o The heating and air-conditioning systems and their ages

  - o All cabinets, doors, windows, and screens

  - o Fireplaces and wood-burning stoves to ensure that they are clean, in good working order, and in compliance with all building codes

- o The major appliances in the kitchen and laundry room if they are included in the purchase

- **Make an offer on the house and have the purchase contract written.** The contract consists of

  - o The Offer—how much the buyer will pay for the house

  - o The Acceptance—that the seller agrees to sell the house for the price offered by the buyer

  - o The Consideration—also known as "earnest money." This is the money that accompanies the contract as a demonstration of the buyer's good faith. It makes the contract binding and precludes the seller from selling the house to another buyer. The earnest money may be refundable within a specified period of time if this is included in the contract.

  - o The contract length—how long the offer is good for. While each state determines the length of time between the offer of the contract and the closing of the sale, 45 days is not unusual.

  - o The real estate disclosures—a written statement made by the owner in which any known defects must be disclosed

  - o The closing date—the date by which the sale must be concluded

- **At closing, compare the Good Faith Estimate to the HUD-1 Statement,** the final statement of all costs associated with the loan, and determine if any of the terms or amounts have changed. If they have, ask for a full explanation before signing the loan documents.

## The Real Estate Attorney

There is no requirement that you have an attorney represent you in the purchase of a house, or that you have one review the contract for purchase. However, since the purchase of a house may be the biggest purchase anyone will ever make, it may be a good idea to hire a real estate attorney. As your legal counsel, your attorney can review important documents like the deed, the bill of sale, the legal description of the property, the loan documents, the plat of survey, the title, and the title insurance policy to make certain that all documents are in order. Your attorney may also be able to help you negotiate any prorated expenses like condominium assessments or homeowners association dues. Your attorney should also attend the closing where everything is finalized.

## Down Payment Assistance Programs

Many states, counties, and municipalities offer down payment assistance programs to first time home buyers, and, in some instances, to workers in specific professions such as police officers, fire fighters, and teachers.

If you believe that you may be eligible for these programs, check with the state, county, or municipal housing authority; or talk with a mortgage loan officer who specializes in these programs.

## CONCLUSION

The decision to purchase a house is not one that should be undertaken lightly. Clearly, there are advantages and disadvantages to both renting and owning.

- Advantages of Renting

    o   You're not tied to one place. You can easily move as you learn more about the area.

- o The landlord is responsible for fixing things when they break.

- o The landlord pays the taxes.

- Disadvantages of Renting

    - o The resident builds no equity. There is no increase in net worth.

    - o The resident cannot readily make changes to the property such as change interior colors or flooring.

- Advantages of Owning

    - o Interest paid on the mortgage loan is tax deductible.

    - o Equity is built and net worth is increased.

    - o You can repaint, change flooring and landscaping, and remodel whenever you want to do so.

- Disadvantages of Owning

    - o It's not easy to accumulate the funds needed for the down payment and closing costs.

    - o When something breaks, you are responsible for fixing it.

    - o Moving may require first selling your current home before purchasing the next one.

Only you can decide which is more advantageous to you. Once you make the decision to buy, there are questions you need to answer.

- What kind of house do you want—single family, condominium, townhouse, duplex?

- Do you want to buy a brand new house or one that a current owner is selling? Again, there are advantages and disadvantages to both courses of action.

- Are you really ready to buy? Do you have

  o Money for the down payment and documentation to verify it?

  o Cash for closing costs?

  o Stable income and steady employment for the past two to three years?

  o The ability to pay the mortgage, interest, taxes, insurance, and perhaps private mortgage insurance, monthly?

  o A good credit history?

  o The ability to pre-qualify for a mortgage loan?

Next you have to choose the right mortgage loan for your situation. Your options include

- Conventional loans

- FHA loans

- Loans available through the Veterans Administration

- USDA/Rural Housing Loans

- Balloon loans

- Construction loans

- Construction-to-permanent loans

Once you receive the appropriate loan, you'll begin making payments. Typically, the payment consists of four components, often referred to as PITI.

- Principle

- Interest

- Taxes

- Insurance

If your down payment is less than 20 percent of the purchase price (and most are), your lender will require that you purchase private mortgage insurance (PMI) that protects the lender in the event that you default on the loan. The cost of this insurance will be built into your monthly mortgage payment, too, if its full cost was added into the loan amount.

Know the possible types of mortgage fraud that you could encounter.

You may choose to retain someone to help you in your search for the right house, a real estate agent. You'll want to make certain that this person is a buyer's broker to ensure that he or she is truly representing your best interests.

When you find your "dream house," you'll want to take all of the proper steps during the purchase of it.

- Determine a fair price for the house

- Have a pre-purchase home inspection performed by a licensed, professional inspector

- Make an offer and have a contract of sale written that includes your consideration (earnest money)

Because a contract is a legal document, you may choose to hire a real estate attorney to ensure that the contract does not contain clauses that are detrimental to you.

If you are a first time homebuyer, you may be eligible for a down payment assistance program. Your real estate agent or your mortgage loan officer should be able to help you determine which programs, if any, you are eligible for.

# Conclusion

Being smart with money isn't rocket science. It's planning ahead, considering alternatives, and making well informed, "wise" choices in how you use your money. The primary goal of this book has been to provide you, the reader, with the information that empowers you to ask the right questions and differentiate good answers from mere salesmanship; to give you the tools needed to make wise spending decisions and obtain the best value for your hard-earned dollars.

Chapters 1 through 4 focused on income and where it can be stored for future use.

In Chapter 1—Budget

- We decided that budget is a four letter word. It is a plan for how to use our money to obtain the greatest value from each expenditure.

- We recognized that while gross income may be more impressive, only net income can be spent.

- We acknowledged that expenses fall into these three categories: fixed, variable, and periodic.

- We acknowledged the difference between "gotta-have-its" and "wanna-have-its"; needs versus wants.

- We recognized that for savings to occur, we must make it a priority and ensure that it occurs every month.

- We concluded that we need to implement a system for controlling spending; a system that works best for each of us as individuals.

In Chapter 2—Saving For...

- We found that there is a multitude of reasons why people choose to save. They can be either

    o   Occasional or leisure expenditures

    o   Large lifetime expenditures

- We discussed the various methods people use to set funds aside for savings.

    o   Payroll deductions and direct deposits

    o   Automatic transfers from checking to savings

    o   Collecting coins in a jar

- We touched briefly on the ways in which banks and credit unions are similar and the ways they differ from each another.

In Chapter 3—Managing Payroll Deductions

- We reviewed the different taxes that are withheld from each paycheck; some of which we can control and others which are fixed by law.

- o Federal Income Taxes can be controlled by the number of exemptions claimed on Form W-4

- o The Earned Income Tax Credit (EITC) is a tax credit given to individuals who are employed at low wages.

- o Social Security and Medicare taxes are set by law

- o The majority of the states have a state income tax

- We delved into the various employer sponsored benefits for which premiums and contributions can be deducted.

- We investigated different tax credits available and how they can increase spendable income.

- We concluded that Flexible Spending Accounts make it possible for the employee to pay certain expenses with untaxed money, with certain caveats.

In Chapter 4—Establishing a Banking Relationship

- We reviewed the characteristics of banks and credit unions.

- We examined the services provided by these financial institutions.

  - o Checking and Savings Accounts, including how to write a check, balance the account, and how important it is to balance the account every month

  - o Safe Deposit Boxes

  - o Certificates of Deposit, including how they differ from a savings account

  - o Credit Cards

o Debit Cards

o Mortgage and Consumer Loans

o Direct Deposit, On-Line and Telephone Banking

o Pre-paid gift cards (stored-value cards) are "loaded" with a set amount of money that the user can then use to make purchases.

- We recognized who the key employees are at these financial institutions and how the job that each one performs is important to us.

Chapters 5 and 6 focused on basic living expenses.

In Chapter 5—Housing, Transportation, and Utilities

- We found that housing costs do not stop with rent or mortgage payments. They can include property taxes, insurance, maintenance, and sometimes association dues.

- We acknowledged that transportation costs are not limited to car payments. They include the costs of purchasing the vehicle, fuel, maintaining the vehicle, renewing license plates, and, in some locations, fees for using toll roads.

- We recognized that some utilities such as water, electric, and natural gas and propane are essential. Others, such as having cable or satellite television, and having both landline and cell phone are discretionary. Managing these expenses is often a combination of conservation and recognizing the difference between wants and needs.

In Chapter 6—Fine Dining on a Budget

- We became aware that the key to resisting the siren songs of creative grocery marketers is to have a plan.

o   We established that such a plan includes

 o   Using coupons

 o   Buying what's on sale

 o   Buying In bulk

 o   Noting and taking advantage of store sales cycles

 o   Using other print and electronic resources

 o   Purchasing non-food goods at dollar-pricing stores when they offer greater value

- Planning meals ahead, shopping wisely, and putting meals together wisely—all are keys to maintaining not only a healthy food budget, but a healthy diet, which in turn may help keep health care costs down.

Chapters 7 through 10 addressed the subject of risk management.

In Chapter 7—Insuring Your Home and Its Contents

- We learned that property insurance protects our homes against losses, whether the dwelling is a home, condominium, apartment, or duplex, and whether you are an owner or a renter.

- We acknowledged that property insurance policies are comprised of different coverages, each designed to protect various parts of the property.

o   Coverage A protects the structure.

o   Coverage B safeguards the outbuildings.

o   Coverage C replaces the contents.

o   Coverage D pays for alternative housing when the structure cannot be occupied.

o   Coverage E provides liability protection when someone is injured on your property.

o   Coverage F pays the medical bills for someone who is injured on your property.

o   Endorsements can be added to the policy to help the property owner recover from a loss as near painlessly as possible.

- We looked at the factors that impact the cost of coverage; thus, these risk factors should be considered when choosing where to live.

In Chapter 8—Automobile Insurance

- We explored the components of an auto insurance policy.

    o   We learned that liability coverage (bodily injury and property damage) protects us against the financial damages that are incurred when another person is injured or another person's property is damaged in and accident that is our fault.

    o   We found that some states, "no-fault" states, require policy owners to carry Personal Injury Protection (PIP) to pay medical costs when we are injured in an accident.

Other states require policy owners to purchase medical coverage as a part of their policy, again to pay medical expenses resulting from an injury suffered in the accident.

o   We discovered that collision and comprehensive coverages pay for repairing the vehicle. Which coverage pays is determined by the cause of the damage to the car.

o   We found that an Uninsured Motorist endorsement can protect us when another driver causes an accident and has inadequate or no insurance.

o   We were pleased to learn that our insurance can provide a rental car for our use if we have purchased Loss of Use/ Rental Car Coverage.

o   We came to understand that Towing and Labor Coverage pays for roadside assistance, but that we need to take care that using this endorsement does not constitute a "claim" against the policy.

o   Gap Insurance protects us from financial loss when the car is declared to be a total loss but is worth less than the amount owed on the loan.

• We looked at the factors that affect insurance premiums and how we can control some of those factors. These factors can include

o   The policy limits chosen

o   The deductibles chosen

o   Moving traffic violations

o   Avoiding frivolous or minimal claims

- A person's credit history

- The vehicle symbol which is a numeric expression of the type of vehicle (the lower the number, the less risk of loss)

- The type of parts that can be used to repair the vehicle

- Shopping wisely for a good company and agent

- Checking with state regulators about complaints that may have been filed against either the company, the agent, or both

- Asking an independent agent to help you compare many companies to get the best value

- We concluded that liability coverage is very inexpensive and that the wise consumer buys as much as possible since the price difference between the "bargain basement" and the "luxury penthouse" liability coverages is seldom more than pennies a day.

- Finally, we learned what to do and what not to do in the event of an accident.

In Chapter 9—Life and Disability Insurance

- We learned that the purpose of life insurance is to protect beneficiaries who survive the death of an insured person, perhaps the breadwinner, who has designated them to receive benefits. While a human life is priceless, the concept of human life value attempts to determine the lifetime earning power of the breadwinner. The life insurance need is determined through the concept of income replacement plus

- Final expenses such as funeral and burial bills

o   Funds needed to pay off debts

o   Replacement of bread winner's income

o   Funds to pay for children's educations

o   Charitable bequests

o   Pension maximization in retirement

- We found that there are different types of life insurance—

    o   Term insurance maximizes the insurance provided while minimizing the cost.

    o   Permanent insurance such as whole life, universal life, and variable life insurance provide insurance protection with a cash accumulation component that can provide living benefits when the insurance protection is no longer needed.

- We developed a method that each of us can use to determine the amount of life insurance we really need based on how we want to provide for our loved ones, the expenses that we choose to incur, and the causes that we wish to support even after our passing.

- We found that while money pays the insurance premiums, good health is what enables a person to buy it; that underwriters review a person's health history to determine if the company is willing to provide the insurance protection requested.

- We were very happy to learn that life insurance benefits are free from federal income taxes when paid to a named beneficiary. They may, however, be subject to federal and/or state estate taxes.

- We discovered that disability can be defined in different ways.

o The inability to perform the duties of one's own occupation

o The inability to perform the duties of any occupation for which the person is qualified based on education, training, and experience

o The inability to perform the duties of any occupation

- We also found that there is a significant difference between a policy that is "non-cancellable and renewable" and one that is "guaranteed renewable."

- We learned that disability income benefits may be taxable or may be tax free depending on who pays the premiums and if the premium dollars are subject to income tax.

Chapter 10—Medical and Dental Insurance

- We found that how and what the insurance pays is often determined by how the policy is structured,

o A point of service plan

o A preferred provider organization

o A health maintenance organization.

- The Children's Health Insurance Program (CHIP), started in 1997, provides low or no cost health care to children who meet certain financial guidelines. Each state administers its own CHIP.

- We were reminded that prescription drug coverage is often divided into three categories which determine how much the policyholder will pay for the prescription.

- o The newest name brand drugs usually have the highest co-pay

- o Older name brand drugs that are still under patent protection typically have a moderate co-pay

- o Generic drugs almost always have the lowest co-pay

- We reviewed some options that people can use to control how much they pay for prescription medication.

- o Use mail-order fulfillment to reduce costs for maintenance drugs

- o Fill prescriptions for more than one month at a time

- o Split pills if your physician approves it

- o Ask your doctor for samples provided by the pharmaceutical representative

- o Ask your doctor if there is a generic drug that works as well as the name brand that was prescribed

- We discussed various ways to reduce the cost of over-the-counter medications.

- o Buy in bulk

- o Use store brands

- o Look for and use coupons

- We concluded that the cost of medical care can be to some extent controlled by the person who is an active participant in the health care process and who looks for ways to manage those costs.

Chapters 11 through 14 revealed how a person can develop plans for long-term financial security.

In Chapter 11—Retirement Planning

- We examined the 4 critical components of retirement planning:

  o Plan

  o Money

  o A way to make money grow

    ➢ Individual Retirement Accounts (IRA)

    ➢ Roth IRAs

    ➢ Employer plans

      ▪ 401(k) programs

      ▪ 403(b) plans

      ▪ 457 plans

      ▪ Many others

- Time

- We explored the concept of risk and how risk determines the opportunity for gain and the possibility of loss.

- We took a high level look at where retirement funds can be invested and how risk is a factor when selecting from the many choices.

- We studied how the time frame within which these funds will be needed can impact the amount of risk that we can afford to take with these funds.

In Chapter 12—Preventing Identity Theft

- We considered the fastest growing "white collar" crime in the country today, identity theft. We studied the myriad ways in which identity thieves obtain an individual's personal, non-public information in order to assume that persona.

  o Dumpster diving

  o Skimming

  o Changing addresses

  o Stealing wallets, credit cards, mail

  o Pretexting

  o Hacking

  o Phishing

- We looked at the steps a person should take when he or she believes that his or her identity has been stolen.

- We reviewed the steps that a person can take to protect against identity theft.

    o  Refuse credit and debit cards containing RFID chips; or shielding the cards to prevent the transmission of account data

    o  Shred documents containing identifying information

    o  Protect social security numbers

    o  Know whom you're dealing with

    o  Avoid simple, easily guessed passwords; make them difficult to guess

    o  Keep passwords secure

    o  Monitor credit reports on a regular basis and take immediate action when something appears to be wrong

    o  Pay attention to see that bills arrive on time

- We acknowledged that routinely reviewing your credit report is prudent, and that doing so can help a person put a stop to the use of one's good name for a bad purpose.

In Chapter 13—Credit Scores and Reports

- We looked at many of the aspects of life that are impacted by a person's credit history.

- We examined two frequently used credit scores and the factors that are considered in the computation of those scores.

    o  FICO Scores

    o  Vantage Scores

- We defined good credit scores and less than desirable credit scores.

- We discussed how to establish a "good" credit score, how to raise a "bad" credit score, and factors that cannot be used in the calculation of a credit score.

- We considered strategies for rebuilding a damaged credit history.

- We reviewed the options that a person has when overwhelmed by debts.

  o   Pay the debt in full

  o   Settle for less than full balance

  o   Seek help from a credit counseling agency

- We explored how credit counseling agencies may be able to help a person overwhelmed by debt and many of the factors that should be considered when selecting an agency.

- We studied the different ways to obtain a current copy of your credit report, how to read that report, and your rights under the Fair Credit Reporting Act if your report contains inaccurate information.

In Chapter 14—Home Ownership

- We compared the advantages and disadvantages of renting (or leasing) vs. the advantages and disadvantages of homeownership.

- We looked at the different types of houses that a potential buyer can choose from.

- o Single family dwelling

- o Condominium

- o Town house

- o Duplex

- We discussed the advantages and disadvantages of buying an existing home or purchasing a new home that has never been occupied.

- We considered the factors that determine if a person is ready to become a homeowner.

- We explored the different types of home mortgages that are available and the components of a typical mortgage payment along with down payment assistance programs that may be available.

  - o Conventional loans

  - o FHA loans

  - o Veteran's Administration loans

  - o USDA/Rural loans

  - o Balloon loans

  - o Construction loans

  - o Construction to permanent loans

- We examined the components of a typical mortgage loan payment

- o Principle

- o Interest

- o Taxes

- o Insurance

- We talked about private mortgage insurance (PMI), which protects the lender in the event of default.

- Because there are unethical people in the world, we examined different types of mortgage fraud and steps that we can take to protect ourselves against these fraudulent behaviors.

- We researched the traits that should be considered when selecting a real estate agent and the role of the agent in the shopping and buying phases of becoming a homeowner.

- We listed the actions that are part of the purchase process.

  - o Determine a fair price

  - o Have a pre-purchase inspection

  - o Make an offer

  - o Have a contract of sale written and pay consideration (earnest money)

- We considered the advisability of having a real estate attorney and his or her role.

- We learned that for a first time homebuyer who qualifies, there are down payment assistance programs.

## Last Words

Throughout history, men and women have looked back over their lives and thought "if only..."

- If only I'd had the tools...

- If only I'd known then what I know now...

- If only I'd done things differently...

You now have the financial toolbox that was never given to you when you were in school. You now know the financial facts of life that you may not have known before. You have the choice of continuing to manage your personal finances as you always have; or you can use the knowledge gained to make different choices, to do things differently. You have the fully loaded toolbox that empowers you to build the financially secure life you've always dreamed of. Now it's up to you to make the choices that can make a difference. It's up to you. Choose wisely.

"It is a most mortifying reflection for a man to consider what he has done, compared to what he might have done."

- Samuel Johnson
In Boswell's Life of Johnson, 1770